uel Beckett's work "that the author himself lies at the heart of his every writing, spinning out a horrendous tapestry that both hides and depicts the wastes of being." Genet is seen by Professor Grossvogel as the congenital playwright, forced by the circumstance of his own complexity to construct and define himself on the stage before his accuser—the spectator—who, in the process, cannot remain "uncontaminated" or unmoved.

These four "blasphemers" represent *the* major forces in the modern theater. As such each receives exhaustive and penetrating treatment. Professor Grossvogel's astute insights into their character and work are certain to stimulate readers interested in contemporary theater and literature. In his Postscript, he suggests what their experiments portend for future drama, extending and genuinely deepening the ideas about actor and spectator which appeared in his earlier book, *The Self-Conscious Stage in Modern French Drama,* in an attempt to formulate an esthetics of the modern stage.

DAVID I. GROSSVOGEL is an Associate Professor of Romance Literature at Cornell University. He received his B.A. degree from the University of California at Berkeley, and the M.A. and Ph.D. from Columbia University. His previous teaching positions have been held at Columbia where he was Managing Editor of *The Romanic Review* from 1954-1956, and at Harvard University. His book, *The Self-Conscious Stage in Modern French Drama* (1958) has been reprinted in paperback as *Twentieth Century French Drama.* He has supplied the introduction and critical notes to an American edition of Jean Anouilh's *Antigone,* published in 1959, and has been a frequent contributor to learned journals on diverse aspects of French literature.

Four Playwrights
and a Postscript

Four Playwrights and a Postscript

Brecht ✧ Ionesco
Beckett ✧ Genet

By DAVID I. GROSSVOGEL

Cornell University Press
Ithaca, New York

© 1962 by Cornell University

CORNELL UNIVERSITY PRESS

First published 1962

Library of Congress Catalog Card Number: 62-17817

PRINTED IN THE UNITED STATES OF AMERICA
BY VAIL-BALLOU PRESS, INC.

A Steven et Deborah

ce qu'en laisseront les censeurs

Acknowledgments

MY sincere thanks go to Mr. Robert Davril and the Fulbright Commission for one year's grace during which to see these plays and write about them.

To Professors Robert M. Adams, Paul de Man, and Peter Demetz I should like to express my deep appreciation for their scholarly insight and their courage in helping me through rocky parts of the first draft, even in the knowledge that my thanks might make them appear to be accessories after the fact.

I would also like to record my debt to Professor M. H. Abrams for his assistance in helping me span the gap between manuscript and book and to Dr. Jean Parrish for her aid in turning the first version into something more readable.

D. I. G.

Ithaca, New York
January 1962

Contents

Introduction

THE four playwrights considered here have in common an aggressiveness: each has come to the theater in his own way, but with anger. Every age expects its theater to be oracular, but age and oracle lapse sooner or later into familiarity. When this occurs, a blasphemer rises to voice his indignation at this meretriciousness, castigating with equal contempt and little logic the stage that allows such familiarity and the public that is content with such meretriciousness.

Whether they felt life to be genuinely intolerable or whether it was merely fashionable to feel that way, these four authors were outraged by life as their society accepted it; and eventually, they were outraged by the human condition itself. Part of the evidence of a corrupt world was a corrupt stage. When they turned to the theater, it was not only in order to find a platform from which to speak the words of their revolt, but to find an expression whose very form might be that of their subverting anger.

These four have been blasphemers. In the case of the first two, opposition was once the very prefix to their work. Eugène Ionesco termed the first writing to bring him fame an "antiplay"; Bertolt Brecht defined the whole of his esthetics as "anti-Aristotelian." The anger of these playwrights invites conclusions *ad hominem:* was not each an alien in his society? Within a non-Communist world, Brecht wrote the majority of his plays as a Marxian apologist. Of the three who generally write their plays in French —and in France—two are expatriates, the Rumanian Eugène Ionesco and the Irishman Samuel Beckett. The only born Frenchman in the group, Jean Genet, claims other allegiances; he has said that he is "a pederast and a criminal" with enough of pride for Sartre to see in his assertion an existential ethics.

There is some merit to the biographical argument. It is true that in a sense each of these authors has been an alien. But each was an alien through artistic necessity, through the need of the poet to see the familiar as unfamiliar; he was alien through his need to be disengaged, if only inasmuch as the one who interprets and records must disengage himself in order to comprehend—to take in and to understand. Even in the moment of their commitment, these playwrights have been disengaged, and it is this fundamental detachment that supposes a conscious alienation of a sort that cannot be completely accounted for by the mere being of the foreigner, the party-liner, the invert. It is doubtful, moreover, whether a biography—the record of things done —ever yields a creator equal to his creation. It is not always easy to distinguish in Brecht at what point the political dialectician is distinct from the lover of dialectic, the advocate of revolution from the scorner of bourgeois stereotypes, the Communist apologist from the nineteenth-century idealist. The "anti" definitions which Brecht and Ionesco give of their theater develop to the leeward side of playwriting; to look for the foreigner in Ionesco is to neglect the purveyor of the official theater of the Fifth Republic. The stifling feeling to which the French plays of Beckett give voice must have come to him first in Ireland;

it is the metaphysical claustrophobia that drove so many of his fellow writers from their homeland in the mistaken belief that their inner torment had geographical boundaries. The antisocial will of Jean Genet comes closest to informing both author and craft—but a cursory examination of the criminal and the pervert Genet would not reveal his esthetics or, hence, much about his theatrical genius.

In 1934, during the early years of the Nazi scourge, Brecht wrote a pamphlet entitled *Five Difficulties in Writing the Truth,* concerning the courage that such writing required, the discernment needed to recognize the truth, the art of turning it into a weapon, the judgment and the cleverness to seek out its likeliest propagators, the means of likeliest propagation. These five difficulties of Brecht explain something about the man; they also help to explain his concern that art preserve utilitarian ties with man. These "difficulties" will be Brecht's when he writes plays even after the end of Naziism (the work was reprinted in 1949); they provide fixed points that place the drama of Brecht in relation to his concerns, and they help plot an aspect of his creative process. The playwrights represented here illustrate a number of the difficulties involved in playwriting (when playwriting is more than pandering), and, as such, they aid in plotting a part of the esthetics of the present theater.

The blood of shrewd Baden peasants was in Brecht's veins—it is doubtful that he ever put communism ahead of his self-seeking, and, as his life was largely in the theater, his self-seeking is essentially a quest for theater. To that extent, biography and the dramatist's craft are indeed related in Brecht. At another level of interpretation, history elucidates Brecht because he felt himself to be a conscious part of it and because, as a thinker and a playwright, it was uppermost in his mind—whether he was telling anew an old Chinese legend or an Elizabethan tale. Whereas Ionesco, Beckett, or Genet acknowledge a moment of history only as an occasional image of their anguish, Brecht is conscious of his position and his responsibilities to a public born of the same moment. Moreover, the books are closed on him: his work is henceforth a totality in time.

But whatever his importance as a witness of his times, Brecht would not be included here if this were his only claim to the theater. As a man of the theater, Brecht is more important as the witness to his own difficulties in witnessing. His dramatic career is shaped by two important lessons. The first is that no art, no lasting creation, arises adventitiously. A long road stretches between *The Caucasian Chalk Circle*, written during and after the Second World War, and *Baal*, written after the First. The earlier work he himself later termed a "dramatic biography," referring both to the "presocial" nature of the play, whose analysis for once encompasses only a single figure and its development, and to the similarity between the twenty-year-old Brecht and the primitivistic earth-god Baal, the guitar-toting, tavern-haunting poet whose cynical self-assertion was expressed in violent and lyrical verse spat out against every form of bourgeois values. Brecht's second lesson was learned more slowly and was never assimilated fully. This was the fact that it is not possible for a single artist to subvert completely traditional forms: every ancient art looks too much like man, is too much a part of that humanity with which it has aged. The dramatic vision of Brecht was most likely too revolutionary, often demanding the assimilation of forms so unfamiliar as to require, in theater and spectator, mutations out of proportion with the gains to be derived from that assimilation.

The writings of Bertolt Brecht are sufficiently varied to deter future critics from effortlessly draping upon him the mantle of greatness. And it is generally acknowledged that his dramatic theory cannot be applied to the letter. But Brecht left the theater something more important than his theories: caught between the demands of the stage and his demands as a stage maker, his plays are occasionally tense with a vibrancy that is evidence of their present life and an assurance of their life to come.

A few years ago, one of England's angry young men, Kenneth Tynan, who had used Ionesco as a battering ram, awoke one day to the realization that he had gotten hold of a lamb. And when, in an *Observer* article, Tynan prodded the mild-mannered French clerk into taking a hard look at social realities, Ionesco disclaimed any brief against "real society" as distinct from the "social machinery."

Ionesco is justified in leaving the intricacies of the social machine to specialists, while concentrating on the imponderables of man. But his very dedication to these imponderables follows rather distantly upon a much more immediate, and superficial, view of the human condition —a view according to which the dilemma of man is merely incongruous, more worthy of spoof than sorrow, more a canard than a serious concern. When he writes his "antiplay," Ionesco is indulging less in an antisocial gesture than in expressing amusement or mild annoyance at the asinine. It is this fun and this annoyance which accounted for the impetus of Dada and surrealism, long before the theories and the constructs of the latter came into being. For the playwright Ionesco, the "difficulty of living" is not as closely related to the problems of "real society" as he would have us believe; instead, the sources of that difficulty are to be found in the theater, since he too has had to learn, though perhaps a little less consciously, the lessons which his craft taught Brecht. Ionesco must now reconcile those dramatic convictions or necessities that lead from the writing of an "antiplay" at the start of his dramatic career to those which, in 1960, allow his *Rhinoceros* to enter the subsidized Théâtre de France. Although Ionesco's disclaimer intends to show that his drama no longer subverts bourgeois clichés but expresses instead the difficulties involved in retaining an essential self within the world of those clichés, his statement must be looked upon, within the articulation of a modern drama, as that of a man coming to grips with certain dramatic problems and solving them, of a playwright gradually sinking into the realities of a theater world that has become an important part of his expression.

Beckett and Genet have transposed, each in his own way, the very substance of their being onto the stage. Whereas the biography of Brecht is caught up in his playwriting to the extent that both are part of the same historical evidence, one feels truly reluctant to question Beckett's private life, so overpowering is the sense that the author himself lies at the heart of his every writing, spinning out a horrendous tapestry that both hides and depicts the wastes of being. Death is the most important part of this mask that looks so much like what it is disguising; but it is present in the only form that has meaning for man—that which starts its infection at birth. It is that death which never comes and which is never absent, the long, agonizing wait. It is the single assertion of Beckett's plays until such a moment as the construction upon the endless sands grows into something more than the automatic talk of desperate men and becomes, perhaps, the single volition of which man is capable while waiting to die. It remains as the handiwork of the artist—the plays that will transmit the desperate voice of an age.

The lifeblood of Genet also flows through his writing, but not in order to animate the statement of a failure. Since he was a young boy, Genet lived the vagrant's life of crime and exclusion, but this state was never natural. He objectified at all times the unromantic dream of his being, contrasting that which he knew he was and that which he knew as well but was not. He has been since early adolescence the conscious negative of the generally accepted positive. Amidst criminals and perverts, he found his truths: that society stifles the life which it shields, while those who savor life must define it every moment of their being; that the outcast's world of suffering and blood, the usual darkness of society, has for those who know it a dark but profound radiance. Genet, the fallen angel, the invert, has always been on a stage, that focus of irreality as real as the living actor and the living spectator between whom it develops—the stage that is not the world of everyday life and yet is a part of it; the stage that is peopled by those who disguise themselves in order to be what they are; the stage that is not life and yet is nothing else. That toxin which Genet brought to the theater was first in his own blood.

In the theater, Genet has been concerned not so much with spitting in the constant eye beyond him that names and accuses him, as with defining his own complexity of being, a complexity that contaminates even his spectator, much in the same way as he was forced to define himself in the face of his circumstances, his sex, and his soul throughout an existence that made of him a playwright before he ever entered the theater.

These four have been blasphemers, but their blasphemy has been in the theater, and it is with the form and the reasons for their irreverence that this writing is concerned. The stage will never be the didactic object of Brecht, the parlor tricks of Ionesco, the silence of Beckett, the mirror game of Genet; but all are dimensions which will be the unmistakable gifts of these dramatists to all future drama. What these dimensions are and how they were conceived by these dramatists comprise the subject matter of the following chapters. The Postscript attempts to relate their experiments to a comprehensive esthetics of the theater. Only the impetus which these writers brought to a changing art form will be examined: important as they are, they have been assembled here only as essential markers. But because they are important, those who are interested in them as dramatists distinct from the evolving nature of drama will be able to find specialized works devoted to most of them (the exception is Genet, still something of an *enfant terrible*) in most of their individual aspects.

One last word. Illustrative excerpts appear here in translation since this work is meant for an English-speaking audience. However, the reader is referred back to the original wherever possible: not only was each of these heretics a poet, in the many meanings of that word (and, as is generally conceded, it is possible to translate of poetry all but that which makes it poetry), but also translations are frequently marred because of expurgations, misinterpretations, or overly cavalier "adaptations." On occasion, even a commonly accepted title has been retranslated to help make a point otherwise lost (either the footnote makes this clear or the text includes the original title). The dates that are given in the text are those of writing, unless specified otherwise.

Four Playwrights
and a Postscript

I ~ BERTOLT BRECHT:

The Difficulty of Witnessing

I am the playwright. I show
What I have seen. In mankind's markets
I have seen how humanity is traded. That
I show, I, the playwright.
  BERTOLT BRECHT, "The Playwright's Song" (1935)

THERE was a time when Bertolt Brecht was living and creating theater in crude form—that is to say, in a raw state, not concocted by the intellect. This happened in the years immediately following the First World War, when Germany was a land in ferment, the pattern of its social texture rent by war, revolution, and economic and governmental prostration. Brecht was back in Munich to resume his medical studies which he had been forced to interrupt during the last year of the war to serve as an orderly in a military hospital. But now, student life was Villonesque, spent in a world of drink and discussion, tavern smoke and whores, art and topical satire of the most wreckless sort, through which Brecht began ballad singing his way, backed up by a guitar or a honky-tonk piano. By 1921, his academic endeavors had ended in this congenial inferno of whisky and wickedness too facile to be wholly credible, whose voice was jazz, whose shrine was the sports arena, and whose exoticism was an Anglo-American idiom that mixed gangsterland and Dixie, Piccadilly and New York, with only casual discrimination or comprehension. The minstrel and his public were one: theater of this sort cannot be better than the moment of which it is exponential; but it is elemental, genuine, and wholly successful.

To theater of this kind, Brecht added another: he began writing plays. *Baal* (1918), his first, was written in disapproval of the sentimentality with which Hanns Johst had written *Der Einsame* (*The Outsider*), a play about the drunken poet and dramatist, Dietrich Grabbe. The drunken poet Baal merely gives a more familiar expression to the *fin de siècle* romanticism to which Brecht objected. Inasmuch as it did little more than place behind footlights the fauna of those tavern times, the play was supposed to rise above an idle display of feeling. But in fact, the special nature of those times was such that they could attain their only reality as a play. None of this made *Baal* any less sentimental: it preserved the familiar guitar, the ballads, the drinking. It added the suicides of lovelorn girls and the murder by Baal of his best friend—gestures that were fated to remain theatrical since it is only gestures such as these that stated the irreality of the footlight world. (The literary source of this incident, the shooting of Rimbaud by Verlaine, indicates another aspect of the playwright's concerns. The artificiality of the author's orgiastic underworld was in part its literariness.)

Written between 1918 and 1920, *Drums in the Night* retains some of *Baal*'s flavor in that it too is a topical play, the mirror of a defeated nation, demoralized and cynical. The contemptuous and drunken hero, Andreas Kragler, is a demobilized soldier whose supreme gesture is his refusal to join the Spartacist fighters of his own class—an enduring skeleton in Brecht's closet. Brecht's protest was too much within the idiom of the times, negating in its sweep even such beliefs as he was later to accept; when the beliefs were accepted, he rejected the play.

In the Cities' Jungle, on which he worked between 1921 and 1924, has been said to anticipate the plays of Beckett and Ionesco, "which it resembles by its insistence on the impossibility of communication." [1] The play tells the story of a scarcely motivated struggle of giants, whose clash is primarily the expression of their size. The setting is exotic; the place, America; the adventurers, the "broad-chested men" of America's steel jungle that were to remain dear to Brecht and that sound an unwittingly nostalgic note in the author's poems published as late as 1951. And once again, the play is a lyrical outcry, part of which is drawn from Rimbaud's *Une Saison en enfer*.

These plays find admirers in those who look for an apolitical Brecht, a dramatist able to make a powerful appeal to the emotions or a pessimistic statement of Aristotelian proportions about the unalterable isolation of man. But in his preoccupation with a more complex esthetics meant for another sort of statement, Brecht moved away from these plays and dismissed them. [2] Since it is the fuller statement of Brecht's esthetics that concerns us here, we must perforce move on with him to the dramatic formulation which he accepted ultimately.

Drums in the Night and *In the Cities' Jungle* were a protest against the mere affection of sentiment (the program note introducing the former began with the words, "Not so much romanticism!"). Brecht's rejection of them in later years was not merely a political gesture; it was also an acknowledgment that romanticism of another sort had somehow crept in. The theorist and the experimenter in Brecht grew out of a lifelong concern to define the nature of this subverting romanticism and to block its access to the theater.

[1] Martin Esslin, *Brecht: A Choice of Evils*, London: Eyre & Spottiswoode, 1959.

[2] See the reference to Brecht's diary notes by John Willett, *The Theatre of Bertolt Brecht*, New York: New Directions, 1959, n. 26.

It was not long before Brecht found a channel and discipline in Marxism for his onslaughts upon the social structure. Brecht began studying *Das Kapital* in 1926. In 1927–1928, being now wholly committed to the theater, he began working with the Communist director Piscator, as well as with lesser-known stage people interested in using the theater as a political weapon. Brecht's *Versuche*, collections of plays, poems, and essays, began to appear in 1930. There were fifteen volumes of the *Versuche* during Brecht's lifetime. The twelfth of these contained in 1953 "A Little Organon for the Theater," which represented a summation and a reconsideration of Brecht's dramatic theory through 1948 (the work was first printed in *Sinn und Form* in 1949). Before the scholars of Brecht themselves turn to the "Organon," they customarily belabor those who base their analysis of his theory on that writing. It is true that the final statement of Brecht must be that of his plays. However, after *The Threepenny Opera* (1928), Brecht became mindful of the extent to which the theorist had been betrayed in the reading and performance by others of his drama. As there is thus at least the possibility that two Brechts existed, it would seem only fair to examine first the one which he himself proposed. Because he wrote nothing of any particular significance after the "Organon," that pronunciamento can be considered sufficiently terminal to be used as a point of departure.

Brecht starts by removing God from the theater: it is the pastime of men amongst themselves, the construction of living images, of events—historical or imaginary—that occurred among men, and, says Brecht, this is done for recreation. Throughout this theoretical writing, he will insist upon these dramatic requisites: the predominance of the spectator and his need to be entertained. This interest in the spectator was not always shown by Brecht; he began his "Marxist" period with a number of so-called "didactic plays" which were meant primarily for the actors. But in 1948, he saw recreation as the main virtue of the stage and one that needs no justification. A "moral" theater is no better than any other; quite the contrary: if it fails to appeal to the senses, it will be worse.

However, amidst the pleasures which the theater can dispense, he distinguishes between weak ones (simple pleasures) and strong ones (complex pleasures). The latter are evident in great drama; they are varied, richer in revelations, more contradictory, and fraught with deeper consequences. Since the masterpieces of bygone days still offer enjoyment, Brecht wonders whether this does not mean that a satisfactory "idiom" is still to be found for the modern theater. Moreover, he believes that the representation of social conditions never has been achieved satisfactorily from the point of view of the modern spectator who is "embarrassed" by what he is shown of it on the stage.

As a Marxist, he feels that the old ways of thinking have not kept pace with the strides of science. Technological progress has altered many patterns, including the relationships of human beings to each other. This interests the theater on two counts, since it portrays such relationships and is also viewed as a scientific tool in furthering man's social evolution. The latter requires a "critical attitude" of the theater which Brecht sees as "engaged," though an unconscious pun defines the nature of that "engagement" —scarcely the existentialists': "The theater must engage itself with reality so that it can and may present effective images of reality." [3]

[3] This and other quotations from the "Organon" appear in the translation by Beatrice Gottlieb, first published in *Accent*, XI,

This reality is one which the spectator must view as a speculative observer, never as a participant. The stage must be a world that is real to the point of recognition—but no more. Brecht takes a strong stand against identification (those who "absorb") which he interprets in a literal way: the becoming by the spectator of a particular person portrayed on stage. He resents the hypnosis through which the spectators are given up to confused though violent impressions. This state of things reverses entirely the dramatic direction that Brecht envisages; traditional tragedy (he cites *Oedipus*) shows the supremacy of the stage, or, from Brecht's point of view, the stage-as-society is stated as not being susceptible to change by the spectator-as-society: "Oedipus, who has sinned against several principles which prop the society of the time, is executed. The gods take care of that; and they are beyond criticism." (Brecht uses the three inept gods in *The Good Woman of Setzuan*, written between 1938 and 1941, to parody this situation.) Brecht wants the spectator to remain lucid; he must, therefore, remain detached. Every natural obstacle in the way of his identification is thus a dramatic good. The playwright is led to seek an "effect of estrangement" ("Verfremdungs-effekt" or "V. effect,") thanks to which the spectator recognizes the stage action, though his "distance" from it makes it appear "strange." This will enable the spectator to see anew social conditions which he had accepted because of too great a familiarity: what seemed hitherto static will appear, in the terms of the Marxian dialectic, susceptible of analysis in function of its "becoming."

no. 1, Winter 1951. All other Brecht translations are identified in footnotes except for quotations from "The Playwright's Song," the song of Baal, and *Notes* to *The Threepenny Opera* whose translations here are the present author's. Original copyright by Suhrkamp Verlag. Production rights with Stephen S. Brecht.

The process requires the elimination of the classical figure whose Aristotelian universality and timelessness allowed indefinite identification. Such a figure, moreover, tended to suggest through its very timelessness the immobility of social conditions and of social strata. Therefore, it should be replaced by figures that are clearly distinguished in the social hierarchy, so that present times also must be recognized as transitory. When the "social motor" changes in accordance with the times, the spectator will find it increasingly difficult to effect identification. This critical distance may also be obtained by depicting contemporary events as if they were remote in history; the circumstances of the action will then no longer be those of the spectator, and he will be able to view that action less subjectively.

Since the "V. effect" actor is not interested in eliciting the identification of the spectator, he himself must not yield to the spell of the part he plays. Being socially conscious and learned, the Marxist actor is in fact a commentator of the action in which he performs. While memorizing his part, the actor should learn by heart his first reactions, his reservations, his criticism, his astonishments, so that they will not be destroyed by "dissolution" in the final creation but will remain alive and perceptible to the public. The actor describes his version of an event. His character is not a necessary incarnation within the action but merely one of its possible forms, so that its very presence becomes a part of the dialectic development of the total performance. Brecht gives evidence of the extent to which he believes that the play is "engaged with reality" by urging his actors to heighten their consciousness through the exchange of roles: "The master is the kind of master his slave allows him to be, etc." (In *Puntila*, 1940, the valet Matti thus becomes more than a character in a play—he is an actual social function. And he is an actor; he has reactions that may not be those of Matti but are a commentary on the function Matti.)

In Brecht's theater, even music is assigned a utilitarian part. It is a mode of expression meant to remain as distinct from the action as the actor and for the same purpose. In the postface to his opera *Mahagonny* (1929), Brecht sets forth some of the functions of music on his stage: it is meant to "explicate" the text, to show a "way of action" (in contrast with Wagnerian music that depicts a "psychological state"). The songs scattered through the plays of Brecht are conceived as separate units that mark a break in the action and invite further commentary upon it. In the same way, choreography is supposed to intensify the stage reality even as it objectifies it: stylization of that which is natural must not abolish that naturalness—it must enhance it. And the list continues (stage design, make-up, costume, and so on) in this theater whose every part is laid under contribution in a single effort to achieve an essential realism and an objective spectator.

The substance of Brechtian drama is the story that is told rather than the Aristotelian persona. The characters themselves resist absorption by the drama; their first objective comment about themselves may occur in their self-introduction, a convention drawn from the Japanese noh and interpreted by Brecht as an exercise in spectator detachment. (He believed that this detachment is basic to all "Asiatic" drama; in fact, the formal statement of the V. effect appears in his theory only after 1935 when he had seen in Moscow the Chinese actor Mei-Lan-Fang.) The first words of Mother Courage are a song that introduces her as a sutler. Pelagea Vlassova introduces herself and the central problem of *The Mother* (1931). In *A Man's a Man* (written between 1924 and 1926), the entrance of Begbick constructs a whole scene, as she presents herself and her "establishment." In the original the whole of *The Caucasian Chalk Circle* (written between 1943 and 1945) is presented as a mere interlude, a play given by an ambulant troupe after the disputants of two collective farms have settled their business. In the didactic play *Die Massnahme* (*The Expedient*, 1930), the process is stylized to the point of barrenness: the four characters take turns playing the parts required by the story in which they have been involved and which they are now narrating and commenting.

The story is told analytically. The play, a sequence of *acts*, is broken down into scenes each of which has its own separate structure; the scenes are tied together in such a way that "the knots are visible" to the spectator, who is thus able to intervene. This accounts for the chorus that frequently anticipates the scene to be played in a Brecht play, as well as the spoken titles which partition the plays —and which, according to Brecht, could preface all stage action. In the words of the "Organon," "Richard Gloucester sues for the hand of his victim's widow"; "God makes a wager with the devil for the soul of Doctor Faust"; and so on. When *The Caucasian Chalk Circle* was first created by the Berliner Ensemble in 1954, Brecht suggested (in an interview given the French newspaper *Le Monde*) that total comprehension of the play—intellectual synthesis as well as mechanical—required the spectator to return several times to the theater. Theoretically, he would focus each time upon another scene viewed through the eyes of another character: the theater is thus a classroom whose lessons depend on a cumulative increase of knowledge and understanding. This intention finds its clearest statement in the plays which Brecht has grouped, as noted, under the heading *Lehrstücke* (didactic plays).

The "story," which Brecht considers the gist of his drama, coincides with the Marxist's concept of the historical determinant. The characters move according to the dynamics of a given moment in history which their acts exemplify. That which was once considered inherent to all mankind and all times—the essential motivation of the classical protagonist—is considered to be merely the result of a particular set of circumstances. Psychological and metaphysical absolutes are no longer prestated. Instead, Brecht believes that the historical process is shaped by man, or, more properly, by the collective body of men, and that individual psychological states—responses to this process—are thus also subject to change and to correction. The Aristotelian figure that filled the classical theater is therefore replaced with the modest performers of a social "gesture" whose cogency and whose significance are determined by the unfolding tapestry which they compose (an image that materializes in the first version of *The Trial of Lucullus*, 1939, as from the general's triumphal frieze witnesses for the prosecution step forward). The classical hero vanishes since *his* gesture is viewed as little more than a summation—a belated summation, in fact—of forces greater than he.

This is not the theater of a single figure. First, there is the independent audience—the autonomous "spectators" who will not become participants in the stage reality. Next, the stage thus erected *before* the spectator functions as the elaborate, architectonic basis for a demonstration—display and proof: this is the so-called epic theater. According to Piscator (in his *Political Theater*, 1929), the term and concept are his. In that the name also came to connote a physical hugeness and a means of ideological suasion, Piscator (himself influenced by Meyerhold) may indeed claim credit for having created an epic theater: the Piscator Theater of the Weimar Republic is still remembered for the magnitude of its productions and a reliance on many sorts of stage machinery that were as a first exaltation of the machine age. But for Brecht, the term does not refer to an esthetic category. Instead, it keeps as its fundamental definition an appeal to reason rather than the senses and refers to the experimental (scientific) techniques warranted to this end. Epic theater it is because, in the manner of the classical epic, it invites reflection rather than participation.

In the postface to *Mahagonny*, Brecht has aligned synoptic tables that contrast the form of the epic theater as he envisages it with that of conventional drama. Whereas the dynamics of the Aristotelian stage work in the direction of absorption (though Brecht sees this absorption effected by the stage rather than by the spectator), the epic form is derived from such principles as will confirm the spectator in his objective detachment from the stage by "awaking" rather than "consuming" his activity. As an intellectual experiment, this drama contemplates tangible attainments while rejecting the claims to transcendence of a former drama: hitherto passive "feelings" will be "decisions"; the former "experience" becomes a specific quest for knowledge.

The spectator is rejected from participation in an action that moves no longer in linear fashion to an attention-centering climax. Instead, he is placed before circular developments of the drama, a series of self-contained units that compel the sustained analysis of a constant movement. The stability of a world based on an assumption of human constants is now viewed for evidence of change whereby to plot the shape of a world to come. The chorus of actors that addresses the public at the start and the close of *The Exception and the Rule* (1930) speaks the lesson of this theater, urging the spectator never to say "it's natural" so that nothing will be thought to be immutable.

It is not through coincidence alone that a number of Brecht's ideas about drama appear as an appendix to an edition of *Rise and Fall of the Town of Mahagonny* (London: Malik Verlag, 1938): the very opera to which the notes are appended can be interpreted as a critique of the sort of drama which Brecht rejects. Mahagonny is a boom-town built for, and thanks to, the money of those who seek pleasure: the opera relates its birth, growth, and death. At a surface level, it echoes Brecht's usual criticism, the exploitation of the many by the few, profiteering, the corruption of justice, and so on. However, the analysis of this escapists' heaven that fails and ends in chaos is also a parable whose moral lesson bears on the meaninglessness of operatic and nonmusical drama alike.

The widow Begbick (the same who had already provided some of the commentary in *A Man's a Man*) defines Mahagonny and its purpose: it is a place of conventional escape, of tinsel paradise and penny exoticism. It has a "green Alabama moon" and a "big and foolish mouth" that laughs.

The principal figure to come to Mahagonny is Paul Ackermann, an Alaskan like all those whose money Mahagonny will drain away. He is typical of many figures in this drama—an illustrative paradigm in an action that affects neither his lucidity nor his incapacity to act in consequence of his commentary. His are prototypical contradictions of the sort that Brecht mentions in the "Organon":

It is an oversimplification to make action exactly fit character and character exactly fit action. The contradictions evidenced by the actions and characters of real people cannot thus be exhibited. The laws of social mobility cannot be demonstrated by ideal cases, since "impurity" (contradictoriness) is inherent in mobility.

Paul Ackermann is a materialist who has to "touch" in order to know whether it is love he feels, but he is nevertheless incapable of acknowledging satisfaction in the tangible pleasures which Mahagonny dispenses. Through the banal praise of his fellow fun seekers, his objection runs as a musical counterpoint: "But there is something missing."

Begbick, one of Mahagonny's cofounders, speaks as the voice of the pandering commercial stage when she considers her own economic problems, for in the first stage of its development, Mahagonny is analogous to the conventional stage: it is a commercial enterprise that provides for its patrons relief from reality in the form of mild sops (whoring and drinking) which appear to the unimaginative to be the height of permissive indulgence. But this toleration is institutional—it is circumscribed by the authority that dispenses it. And so in this incarnation, Mahagonny fails; as an escape, it is too literal an antistatement of reality and too tame.

Thereafter, the idyllic white cloud that symbolized escapist Mahagonny grows into a hurricane and, about to be swallowed up by the tornado, Paul Ackermann discovers the so-called laws of human happiness. But Brecht is being ironic. What Paul has discovered is that the institutionalism that hemmed in his pleasure has become meaningless: he now feels that he can do as he pleases. And when the cyclone bypasses Mahagonny in the convenient way of operetta miracles, Mahagonny's new motto becomes "Everything is permissible on this earth," and four scenes show the mechanistic pattern of this expanded freedom which now includes overeating, love-making, boxing, and drinking.

This second incarnation of Mahagonny is reminiscent of the nihilistic aspects of *Baal.* The difference between these two plays derives from the author's increasingly critical view of his protagonist: the destructive, self-indulgent freedom of Mahagonny ends in chaos and the dissolution of such human contacts as Paul Ackermann had sentimentally aspired to. Paul ends in the electric chair for nonpayment of debts, and remarks that even in this extremity he still has not lived. The joy he bought was not joy, and the freedom he got for cash was not freedom. The curtain comes down on pandemonium, as conflicting groups appear on every side, each clamoring the brazen slogans of its own self-interests.

Mahagonny remained without echo. Yet, two years before its staging, another opera of Brecht's had been a success. *The Threepenny Opera* was an immediate hit in Berlin when first produced in 1928. Brecht was suspicious of the *Opera's* success: for a while the unequivocal *Lehrstücke* were to follow.

As conceived by Brecht, the didactic play draws upon his anti-Aristotelian wisdom (later outlined in the "Organon") in order to create a play of great apparent simplicity. It is in fact a narrative rather than the performance of an action; the actor is a mediator and an obstacle between the role which he performs and the spectator who represents yet another figure in the debate. But the complexity of the relationship between the spectator and the figure on stage is such that the most typical of *Lehrstücke* becomes something more than the simple statement envisioned by Brecht.

The Expedient is such a play. Four political agitators explain to a chorus of party judges why they were forced to kill one of their comrades with his consent. The judges ask them to show the events, their causes. They will then hand down their conclusions. And, in the matter-of-fact manner alluded to, the four actors proceed to play eight scenes relating the events of their mission to China during which they shot and then threw into a lime pit one of their helpers whose intentions were good, but whose acts were bad. Each one of the agitators steps into the parts required for each scene by first introducing himself; he then joins in the action which his words have prepared. In his notes for this play, Brecht has specified that each of the four actors must have the opportunity to show once the behavior of their young comrade because the singers and actors of the play have the task of teaching while they themselves are learning. Thus, all the elements of the didactic play are assembled—the lesson and its commentators and the dissociative devices such as the distant places, the short and self-contained episodes, the action-breaking songs, and so on.

Because this dissociative process attempts to create a theater of judgment, the "V. effect" is felicitously suited to a play set in a courtroom. The spectators are supposed to be sufficiently wise to determine the merits of the questions before them: their remoteness (as judges) from the stage confirms the form of that stage (a courtroom) and the reality of the debate set upon it. However, this balance within the absolute reality of the stage-courtroom is preserved only as long as the dramatic action is limited to the presentation of an intellectual debate. So long as the spectator enters only into an argument (only violence can change this murderous world), the total dramatic reality is a part of his own world and the judges-on-stage are as a mere second audience no different from the one of which he is a part (a kinship intensified by Brecht's command, already noted, that the actor memorize along with his role his own first reactions, his reservations, his criticism). But if this consideration of data should become, through the dramatic process, the performance of an action shown as human reality (the horrified reactions of the executioners to their necessary murder), the judges-on-stage lose their previous autonomy: they are engaged in a dialogue that credits the statements on stage as the evidence of a world to which they belong. The spectator is excluded from this stage world since he is not a participant in the action which is henceforth referred to as accepted reality by the people on stage. In order to effect a repossession of the world, the spectator must credit—through identification this time— the world in which the actors perform as people, and that world includes the stage judges. No longer on an equal footing with the spectator, these judges now derive their reality from his own. The objective criteria for judgment are destroyed by the subjective criteria of the spectator re-creating in his image the reality of these people; the objective demonstration is lost in subjective "absorption."

Through the necessary consequences of his being, the spectator cannot maintain an objective relation to the debate once it is given the extension of a reality other than that of the spectator's immediate, physical circumstances: the spectator cannot create this new world within him on alien terms. Once he is asked to put flesh on the bare bones of a debate, the flesh will usually be his own, seldom the author's. The very nature of the dramatic process is hypnotic. If it were not, Brecht would not have had to devote a lifetime of writing and coaching to neutralize its effects.

Although the theoretical writing of Brecht consistently condemns the negative nature of this "absorption," there is evidence that he accepts its mechanism in his drama. Nearly every play of his, from the earliest, uses this entrapment of the spectator to effect a dramatic—and didactic—dissociation. An opera that satirizes opera, and more generally all forms of drama rejected by Brecht, is an inducement to accept his terms while enjoying the terms which he disparages; it is the playwright's supreme tribute to the lethal seduction of the stage. Only when this seduction has fully operated is he able to shock his spectator into meaningful awareness, such as in the "title" of scene xix in *Mahagonny* when he himself steps onto the stage to suggest that although many spectators will most likely contemplate with regret the execution of Paul Ackermann, few would have consented to pay his debts in order to save him.

Other factors complicate and jeopardize the simple statement of the didactic play. Prophesying the Moscow trials, *The Expedient* conveyed a political message that was easy to read—the need for self-effacement and commitment to an ideological discipline. Piscator had achieved already the sort of *Lehrstücke* that develop an intellectual commentary, using if need be the explicit statements of slides, motion pictures, graphs, posters, statistics, and the like. But Brecht was haunted even in the days of his association with Piscator by the dramatic form of such dialectic, and it is because of this concern that his political themes are shaped by their dramatic form more than by the dialectic process itself. The revolutionary agitators in *The Expedient* are first the tenets of a debate; long-term considerations must prevail over impulses even if they are humanitarian (the agitators enact the compassionate gestures of the comrade whom they will execute, as well as the dire consequences of his tenderheartedness). But this argument— the necessary effacement of self—is contaminated by the stage and changed into something quite different: the dramatic representation of the quest for self.

The "Organon" records these notes:

The ancient and medieval theaters alienated their characters by using masks of people and animals, and the Asiatic theater still uses musical and pantomimic Alienation Effects. These effects undoubtedly prevented empathy: yet the technique rested on hypnotically suggestive foundations rather more than less than the technique by which empathy is produced. The social aims of the ancient effects were entirely different from ours.

Does Brecht succeed in avoiding that hypnotic effect when he uses the mask? The protagonists of *The Expedient* are firstly "faceless men," blank tablets upon which the Revolution impresses its orders. Their facelessness refers to the anonymity of the underground struggle and to self-abnegation before an ideal that humbles individual assertion. The symbolic masks put on by the revolutionaries are simply another layer under which is lost the original man. But in the young comrade there is a fierce need for immediate human contact. He rips off his mask, the nonhuman disguise that has kept him apart from his fellow men. For the first time, a human being—the only one—is revealed on the stage.

At the political level of the play, this action triggers unfortunate occurrences; the identity of the agitators is revealed and their lives are imperiled. They must remove their well-meaning comrade. But even this political conclusion is translated symbolically, and the play gives evidence once again of concerns that singularly extend its didactic statement. The young man is first shot, and then his body is dropped into the lime pits on the outskirts of the city; his human traits will thus be blotted out for good. This preoccupation with the human constants of characters is a strange one for such as were originally supposed to be the figures of a demonstration. Especially for a political henchman, these concerns have little political significance; in fact, they direct attention to the problem of being which inverts the political lesson of the *Lehrstück* (the necessity of nonbeing). The human reality of the dramatis personae defeats the didactic purpose in as insinuating a manner as the human presence in the story destroyed political effectiveness. This follows directly from an innocently subversive statement in the "Organon": "[The theater would be in danger] if it did not make morality pleasurable, that is, pleasurable to the senses."

Since the first dimension of the theater is that of its human performers, the creation of a personal identity is its first concern. Pirandello showed that it was natural thereafter for the stage to explore the complexities of this human factor: the process allowed the theater to reflect upon itself while reflecting upon the condition of man. Brecht, who spent a lifetime in the theater, found it difficult to prevent the dramatic dialectic from informing his political expression—even though the former often worked against the latter. In his drama, the various appearances of a human identity in the flux of time certainly claim equal importance with illustrations of the social condition in the flux of history. Such manifestations are spontaneous drama, and Brecht utilizes them as such, often as visual (that is, naturally theatrical) statements. In *Galileo* (1939; subsequently revised in an English version in 1947 and another German version in 1954), the thin and uneasy cardinal Barberini is transformed on stage, vestment by vestment, into Pope Urban VIII. Galy Gay, the weak and easygoing dock worker in *A Man's a Man*, leaves his shack one morning to buy a fish and is caught up in a sequence of events that change him against his will into a machine gunner of the British army in India. To this the sutler Begbick speaks the lesson as she steps out of character to point out that Bertolt Brecht shows how you can make anything you wish out of a man. Brecht's formal interest in Marxism was taking shape at about the same time as he started work on this first "epic play" (1924) but, as usual, the human undertone of the political statement changes Galy Gay from an abstract example into a human being who moves into the center of the stage and the spectator's intimate consciousness.

Brecht's first drama, *Baal*, has been a reckless expression of self, tempered now and again by fits of romantic anguish. These moments of anguish are the first lineaments—ill-defined and inadequately expressed—of a disparity between self and seeming; that disparity is shown in nearly all the subsequent plays. Puntila is a drunken landowner who refers to his occasional lapses into sobriety as "fits" because at such moments he becomes an evil and unpleasant person. The play, *Puntila and His Valet Matti*, ends when Matti is able to see the face of the coarse exploiter even through the humane mask of drunkenness. *The Good Woman of Setzuan* tells the story of the prostitute Shen-Te, a figure of exceptional kindness on Brecht's boards. In order to hold her own against a brutal world, Shen-Te begins to live a part of her life in the mask of a ruthless "cousin," Shui-Ta, an exact counterstatement of her former being. *The Caucasian Chalk Circle* develops in consequence of the interplay between human surface and substance. Grusha, a farm girl, saves the child of a deposed governor and cares for it as her own. When the governor's wife later demands the return of her child, its identity will be determined by the test of the chalk circle that resolves which of the two women has the more substantial claim to motherhood. People are seldom what they seem to be, on this stage, and though the appearance and its inner contradiction are usually made to point out a political failing, the spectator may justifiably feel anguish in the intimation of a human reality beyond the power of political wisdom to change—at least so far.

This persistency of the self-and-others within the characters of Brecht is presumably a lingering echo of his earlier expressionism. Central to an expressionist drama is a concern with the relation of the self to an external reality which is frequently a subjective statement (the "terrifying semireality about an imaginary creation" of which Strindberg speaks in reference to his own drama). On the expressionists' stage, the hero (who is frequently the author himself) peoples the stage reality with the tangible creatures of his hallucinations (one of the first manifestoes of German expressionism stated: "The real image of the world is within us"). Baal was such a hero; when Brecht rejected him, he rejected the temptation of anarchic self-indulgence in favor of criticism disciplined by dogma. But the fragmentation of the expressionist hero into figures other than his own remained a constitutive element of his later drama.

Whether or not Brecht was conscious of this heredity, he was soon aware that any dramatic statement of illusion and reality through the human presence on stage defies rational analysis and jeopardizes the principles of a theater meant to resist—through analysis—absorption into what Brecht saw as a favorite German Valhalla, the hazy land of generalities "incorporeal and abstract." It is presumably for this reason that his people generally evidence little feeling for their own nonideological problems. Whatever they may have to say about themselves or their relationship to others is less the expression of formless and intimate feelings than the crisp outline of a sociopolitical commentary, the value of which—in terms of historical cogency—reflects the degree of their maturity on this sociopolitical stage. The fundamental detachment on Brecht's stage is that of the human actor *impersonating* a character that consciously evinces the symptoms of a human being.

When the human lure is removed from the mechanical creature on stage, its bloodlessness contrasts with a lusty drama loosing upon these stages colorful masses that portray the turmoil of camp life and soldiery (*A Man's a Man; Mother Courage*, 1939), revolution and upheaval (*The Caucasian Chalk Circle; Mahagonny*), the exuberance of carnival crowds (*Galileo*), the gusto and violence of the underworld (*The Threepenny Opera*, whose development follows closely Gay's *Beggar's Opera*), and so on. In the midst of this life and excitement walk surprisingly thick-skinned or indifferent protagonists—generally sexless women or weak men, passive commentators of an action that affects only their commentary. Although the women are outspoken, the men coarse, and the morals free, there is little sensuality. The women are grotesque in the postures of physical love because of their age (Mother Courage, Begbick) or because the act has been rendered intentionally mechanical (the many prostitutes in *The Threepenny Opera, Mahagonny*, and *Mother Courage*, for example). Or again, the women are young but somehow hard enough to resist the submission implicit in the flesh (Grusha, Shen-Te). It is only in the late *Puntila* that something like a sensual climate develops thanks to the drunken hero, but that sensuality is frustrated by the moral lesson that denounces the falseness of such drunken humanism. Through every woman on this stage, there runs a tough fiber that negates her sex (while Shen-Te, in whom that native toughness is lacking, simply changes into a man—one of the few purposeful males in this drama). By contrast, the men appear to be apathetic and merely talkative. MacHeath, the gangland boss of *The Threepenny Opera*, is a bourgeois who hates the sight of blood and even resorts to the expedient of appropriating his henchmen's crimes. Paul Ackermann (*Mahagonny*) sings a paean to destruction—but pays for the damage he has done immediately afterward (and significantly sings in his great anger a chorus in which recur the words, "Hold me back or I'll do something dreadful!").

The reduction of stage people to mechanical objects makes them comical, and Brecht has consciously allowed this to happen to figures which he deemed to be socially unsatisfactory (such as MacHeath and Ackermann). In the same way, Polly Peachum's failure to confirm her father's description of her ("she is sensuality incarnate") contributes to the comic ineffectualness of old man Peachum (*The Threepenny Opera*). But when the comic context is not justified by the critical position of the author, the mechanical individual voids certain dramatic effects of their intended meaning: blows that signify the oppression of an unenlightened social order rain unconvincingly on such obviously tough hides (as is the case in the bloody beating given to Azdak, the drunken judge who devises the Caucasian chalk circle test). The discursive detachment of the victims reduces the statement of social evils to mere words, and the picture of misery is dissipated in argument —the more so in that Brecht seldom departs from an ironic tone that further lessens the impact of what he is saying, thus calling attention to the detachment of the author. Communist critics themselves have been disturbed by these

forsaken characters that are unable to initiate a gesture
of revolt or do more than comment on vicissitudes which
they endure.

This refusal to acknowledge more than a mental existence is the best guarantee which the character can offer
against throbbing with the spectator's pulse; and although
it does not always insure the sort of drama which Brecht
desired, it resists metabolic stimulation and places the spectator in a position to comment and thus to benefit from that
which Brecht considers the theater's greatest good—its
power to enlighten and teach.

For the sake of instruction, Piscator had made of his
stages the huge and perfected means of conveying a message. Brecht hoped that the dramatic mechanism could be
made to function in the same way as the lecture room, with
merely another dimension, the faculty of representation.
As for critical enjoyment—pleasure without participation
—Brecht thought he had found it in the not-yet-forgotten
sports arenas of his student days and the circus. But Brecht
neglected to consider that the representational dimension
of the stage not only distinguishes it from the lecture platform, but accounts wholly for the mesmeric force which
he wanted to limit. He failed to note that the lecturer is
frequently tempted to enlarge his fact-dispensing function
by *dramatizing* himself, telling jokes, projecting slides,
enacting illustrative material. In much the same way, the
elaborate didactic machine of Piscator sometimes reverted
to merely splendid theater.

Brecht's reference to the "objectivity" of sports and
circus crowds seems to be simply an indication of his pref-
erence for one spell (enthusiasm) over another (maudlin
sentimentalism in drama); the animal and sexual urges
loosed at ringside, the tense enthrallment by acrobats, and

the sexual and scatological evocations of blow dealings and clowns are psychological commonplaces. Such very different analysts of the human predicament as Ghelderode and Rouault have found in the clown an essential persona. Nor is it certain whether Brecht himself believed fully in the objective detachment of sports fans. It will be recalled that in *Mahagonny* one of the unsatisfactory opiates is boxing.

Similarly confused by Brecht would seem to be the psychological process through which the street singer operates. "Epic" distance from the troubadour, as envisaged by Brecht, would signify the troubadour's failure. His success derives from his ability to synthesize most parts of the dramatic ritual: in Europe, the balladmonger spans the bleak years between the last of the Roman theater and the rebirth of a popular theater during the Middle Ages. There is an animal essence missing in Brecht's picture of the "epic" bard surrounded by a soberly reflective audience.

In *A Man's a Man*, Galy Gay is a weak person, "incapable of saying no." It is because he cannot stand up to his fate that he is transformed first into a soldier and ultimately into a blood-craving gunner storming the passes to Tibet. In order to accept Begbick's lesson (you can make anything you wish out of a man), the spectator must accept the indecisiveness and petty self-indulgences of Galy Gay as generally applicable attributes. This dilemma stems from the conflicting demands of Brecht's dramaturgy. It has been noted that although there is an antecedent drama which accounts for the form of the characters' multiplicity, that multiplicity endures in the need to make of this stage an accurate microcosm. "Society should be treated here as though it does what it does experimentally" ("Organon"): the Aristotelian stylization, in which every age recognizes

anew the human quandary, must be replaced by the circumstances of an irrefutable but passing truth, calculated
to awaken in the spectator a merely clinical concern. But
when the social movement becomes the "gestus" of individuals (the fundamental posture of one person in relation
to another, for the sake of meaningful commentary by
a third), Brecht is forced to induce general truths from
particularized statements. He also faces the danger of drawing attention exclusively to the "gestus" and its special
performer at the expense of the social significance and the
patterns for which that "gestus" stands.

To move out of this impasse, Brecht is forced to rely on
the good will and the aptitude of his spectator—and the
demands which he makes on him are sometimes so tenuous
as to seem facetious. The notes concerning the staging of
The Threepenny Opera ask, for example, that when Polly
Peachum takes her place next to MacHeath at the wedding
banquet, the action "show how the betrothed is an object
of general carnal interest just as she is to become the possession of a single owner. At the very moment when the
supply must end, it is natural that the demand should soar
one last time." The implications of such a scene are especially hard to grasp as, at this moment, MacHeath's friends
are slapstick figures parodying bourgeois manners and concerned with the fine points of an etiquette that eludes them
utterly. Moreover, Brecht notes farther on that Polly must
appear as a young girl who is both virtuous and likable
(though the latter refers to the scene in which a business-
like Polly takes over MacHeath's enterprises just prior to
his arrest). Conversely, Brecht asks that in the Pimp's
song the sexual theme be rendered as comedy, "because
the sex life contradicts the social life and because this contradiction is comical inasmuch as it is historical, that is,

capable of being resolved within a different social order."
The spectator envisaged by Brecht thus recognizes these
contradictions as the indications of a "total" person on
stage, but resists them as the intimate and irrational manifestations of his own reality. At no point does Brecht limit
the psychological reality of the stage person to the demands
of a particular historical moment; he merely states "contradictions evidenced by the actions and characters of real
people" ("Organon")—and thereby parallels Aristotelian
universality. He feels nevertheless that the spectator will
be able to objectify that universality within the given historical moment to which it confers its truth, but from which
the spectator will be able to isolate himself.

There is thus ground for suspecting that instead of edu-
cating his spectator through his plays, Brecht requires for
their correct interpretation a spectator who is already fully
educated. This suspicion finds confirmation when one notes
the particular results which Brecht expects of certain dramatic devices. He notes in the "Organon" that the elegance
of a gesture and the charm of a scenic arrangement are
already sufficient to establish "distance." Yet "charm" is
a quality that attracts, and the power of such "elegance"
(stylization which is a "distance" from the natural form)
to preserve this "charm" is the very nature of art—an example of which might be the Aristotelian abstraction whose
rejection, for didactic purposes, Brecht has successfully
argued. It is not unlike the "distance" of the oriental mask
which Brecht accepts while rejecting its suasion, though
he recognizes its "hypnotic suggestion." The "Organon"
mentions a stage set for *King Lear* at the Jewish Theater in
Moscow that was reminiscent of a medieval tabernacle and
"removed" the play. Brecht views this "removal" as a distance calculated to effect the spectator's detachment from

the circumstances of Lear, since these circumstances may
awaken in the spectator familiar stirrings; but he evidently
rejects the dramatic distance that is represented by religious
awe and that, at a level removed from familiarity, links
spectator and performer within the solemn wonder of the
rite.

The impressionable comrade in *The Expedient* hears
coolies singing as they haul rice barges and is moved to
exclaim that although their work is utter slavery they grace
it with the beauty of song. This he finds "horrible!" But
on stage, if that song is beautiful, it is an absolute reality
whose assertion must be stronger than the misery of the
coolies which is merely proposed—the more so, presumably,
in that this music does not express a "mood" but enjoys
"perfect independence" so as to contribute to the intellectual commentary. An exclamation that acknowledges
"beauty" expresses "attachment": it is a dangerous admission in a social theater where villains and victims alike sing.
Significantly, the one who voices that admission in *The
Expedient* must be shot.

Any extension of the human suggestion, whether because
of the psychological conformation of the play or the artistic
statement of the playwright, evokes such preintellectual
"attachment." Every time Brecht gives in to the artistic
temptation, he places his didactic aims in jeopardy. He is
quoted by Eric Bentley as saying, "I have chiefly worked
in the theater. I have always thought of the spoken language." [4] But Brecht is a poet, and the spoken language
of which he has thought is filtered through the Bible (by
his own admission, his greatest linguistic influence), the
Elizabethans, and Goethe. When German vernacular tem-

[4] In the postface to *The Private Life of the Master Race*, New
York: New Directions, 1944.

pers that lyric expression, it is still that of a poet, perhaps
because—as Eric Bentley speculates—it is written in a
language that has not yet been eroded by a literary tradition. Only the heightened speech of *Baal* and its literary
content removed the play from a daily experience that was
largely play living. One wonders thereafter how far the
general pronouncements of Brecht can be trusted. In his
poem to the Danish writer Andersen Nexö, Brecht pre-
dicted that poets will be read by future generations only
for such factual information as they were able to preserve.
Yet it is the history book that properly preserves such facts.
The poem—on paper or on stage—records the fact only
in terms of the human reality that states it. And that reality
exists exclusive of facts which perish sooner than the human
assertion. The songs of Brecht, his stage words, his poems
will not become an objective dialogue between singer, playwright, poet—and the spectator; they have their own life,
tentacular and mysterious as the pagoda of the Yellow God
of Kilkoa (*A Man's a Man*) that seizes the living being that
enters it.

Whatever the intensity of his speculative thought, Brecht
remained fascinated by the fact of the stage. With other
postnaturalists, he understood that the first assertion of the
stage is an assertion of self and is noncontingent. A stage
may show the tread and passage of humanity; but it cannot be a street. (It cannot even show a concern with
streets; at the very most, it might express in its own way
that which a street is.) All through Brecht's lifetime, he
heard Communists insisting that the stage become a mere
platform for documentary evidence; and all the while,
Brecht insisted that the only evidence of the stage is its
own statement at the intersection of fact and figment. And
its mystery held him fast. His analyses of the dramatic

ambiguity, in theory and on stage, he guilefully offered as destruction; they are in fact constructs. Before Brecht, Jean Cocteau had walked upon an authorless stage and watched the electrician bring alive his worlds upon it. With an eighteenth-century conscience, Brecht demanded from the same electrician a stage fully lit to preserve the watchful wakefulness of the spectator—but he also demanded that the lights be visible, and thereby emphasized the statement of the stage. Unaccountably, he also required moons —but specified that they be stage moons, mere moon disks, to show conclusively that there is no real moon over a stage. And yet is not the green and sarcastic Alabama moon of *Mahagonny* the same that once shone quite nostalgically in Munich beer halls? Playwrights with less duplicity (for example, Ghelderode, in *Sortie de l'acteur*) have acknowledged that the moon disk must remain over the stage and on the side of fairyland. Reality is on the other side, within the spectator, the ambiguous respondent to the ambiguous stage—the esthetic animal sensitive to the irreality of the stage even while he informs it with the dimensions of his animal reality. The noh actor, who comes before this spectator as simply another man, does so in order that, as he changes into an actor, he may lead the spectator into that other reality beyond the footlights; it is an oriental courtesy. When Brecht uses the device, is his statement of separation sufficient to subvert it?

Even when the stage is turned by the playwright into a conscious statement of its own irreality, it is doubtful whether it effects the sort of spectator "disengagement" that Brecht desires. In its original form, the entirety of *The Caucasian Chalk Circle* is shown as an interlude—a play put on by an ambulant troupe for the benefit of rival collective farms at the conclusion of a legal argument. This manner of presentation is reminiscent of *The Expedient:* the first actors on stage become the spectators of the play within the play, and their reality contrasts with the objectified performance of the moral lesson. However, the statement of the play within the play is the only significant one here (it is over twelve times as long as the action that introduces it; even Brecht lost interest in his framework). Thereafter, the conventional dramatic suasions take over as the story of a human being, Grusha, unfolds.

The "accent on the break," which the "Organon" demands of the song, may be regarded as a fragmentation of the same technique, a complex instance of which occurs in *The Threepenny Opera* when Polly Peachum sings Jenny's Pirate Song. Polly first calls for cues from those around her, thus transforming the banquet scene into the harbor scene to which the song refers. (It should be noted that the banquet scene itself is false at many levels; it is set in an abandoned stable whose strange festive props are stolen odds and ends that have been arranged in full view of the spectator by the friends of MacHeath, whom this artificiality mocks. They themselves are masquerading as bourgeois in "smart evening dress, but their behavior during the rest of the scene is not in keeping with their attire." [5] When Polly starts, the golden "song lighting" goes on and three pathetic lamps at the end of a stick are lowered: all the false pathos and false magic of prior stages are elaborately mocked. But falseness defines the stage, whatever its means, and its self-mocking can be but the statement of a self-perpetuating truth. And on that stage, even after a character named Polly has been obliterated, there is a

[5] *The Threepenny Opera*, translated by Desmond Vesey and Eric Bentley; in Bentley, ed., *From the Modern Repertoire*, Series One, Denver: The University of Denver Press, 1949.

woman singing. The mockery could not be perceived—
The Threepenny Opera became an international hit.

The sensual immediacy of any stage dims its message; a
didactic theater will find it difficult to attach a specific
meaning to its afferent impulses. The body gropes blindly
toward its triumphs and pains: only the mind can debate
without elation or suffering; the theater allows it hard
entry.

In *Baal* there is sometimes an echo of Brecht's most
intimate poetry:

> When Baal grew in his mother's milky womb
> The sky was then as big, as calm and pallid,
> young and naked and immensely strange
> the way Baal loved it later when Baal came on the scene.
>
> (Song of Baal)

> I, Bertolt Brecht, came from the Black Forest.
> My mother carried me to town while in her womb I lay
> And still the coldness of the woods lingers
> And shall remain in me until my dying day.
>
> ("Concerning Poor B. B.") [6]

And, in conformity with his theoretical views, Brecht later
rejected *Baal;* but there remained the temptation to view
characters from within, even though his characters were
to instance only an intellectual dialectic. Several plays of
Brecht ask the question: "Does man help man?" It is asked
by the chorus in the *Baden Didactic Play on Acquiescence*
(1929) that sits in judgment upon a fallen flyer. His admission that he flew for nothing and for no one will require
his ultimate banishment from among the living. The play

[6] Translated by H. R. Hays, in *Selected Poems* of Bertolt Brecht,
published by Grove Press, Inc., Copyright © 1947 by Bertolt
Brecht and H. R. Hays.

is stark. With the exception of the Reciter's words that have the clipped lyricism of Luther's Bible (the "speech of the market place"), the blank verse is concise and plain; the language of the play is in keeping with its linear action and simple statement. When the chorus casts out the guilty flyer, he is wiped out, like a useless figure on a blackboard; never does he acquire significance other than that of the actions for which he stands. In 1939, Brecht returned to the question formally—an indication of the central position that it occupies in his ethical system. It is formulated this time by the infernal judges in *The Trial of Lucullus* who must determine whether the Roman general was useful to men. But in the latter play, there emerges a human figure within the debate: Lucullus is a man growing progressively less arrogant as his trial proceeds. At the conclusion of the play, Lucullus having been found guilty, mere departure (as in the *Baden* play) is no longer sufficient—he will have to be eradicated from even the dead and "disappear into nothingness." His fate recalls that of the young comrade in *The Expedient* whose sin likewise demanded utter efface- ment as he too had acquired a human face.

But the abiding interest of Brecht in the question of man's social responsibility causes him to pursue it into even more intimate recesses. In *The Caucasian Chalk Circle*, written six years after the first of the *Lucullus* plays, the singer who comments on Grusha's perilous devotion to the child she has saved is moved to exclaim (in the original), "with a ringing voice": "It is a terrible thing/The temptation to goodness!" The problem is no longer debated formally. It is now assimilated within the character of Grusha whose calvary can be linked to the formal lesson only retrospec- tively and at an intellectual level that is remote from the scene of her suffering. The explicitness once devised by

Brecht to formulate the statement of the debate is now made use of by the singer who speaks what Grusha thinks but does not say. Instead of an intellectual formulation, a living person is laid bare before the spectator, and the rational statement becomes dependent on the vicissitudes of the person that replaces it.

Although there is no chorus to express the terms of the problem, it may be inferred as well from the figure of the gentle prostitute Shen-Te (*The Good Woman of Setzuan*) who also absorbs her own morality. As an impersonation of the last vestige of human decency, she is given a reward of a thousand dollars (this was in 1940) by three rather casual gods; but in order to keep the money, she finds it necessary to change into the ruthless Shui-Ta. It is when she falls in love that she fails to heed the wise counsel of Shui-Ta and brings disaster upon herself, only to be left with the irresponsible words of the gods as they drift away on their pink cloud: "Be good and all will be well." But the morality is clear only if it is more compelling than Shen-Te's human dilemma and pain.

The interest of Brecht in the ethical postulate may derive in part from the dramatic problem which it raises. As a moralist, he refuses goodness when it leads to human misery: when the salvationist Johanna finds that God works no miracles in the stockyards, she goes to her death denouncing goodness even though her martyrdom is being turned into a myth for the benefit of the exploiters (*Saint Joan of the Stockyards*, 1930). But Brecht is unable to resolve the quandary. In *Puntila*, ten years later, the last arguer to state an opinon on the practical value of goodness says: "It depends." Biographical analysts of Brecht believe that they have found another reason for this otherwise curious reticence on the

part of an "engaged" social critic; they point to a poem
of his translated as "The Mask of Evil" (although "anger"
would seem to render the German "bös-" more accurately):

On my wall hangs a Japanese carving
The mask of an evil demon, decorated with gold lacquer.
Sympathetically I observe
The swollen veins of the forehead, indicating
What a strain it is to be evil.[7]

But not all the people in Brecht's drama are good. The
Marxian theorem turns upon itself through its imputation
of evil to oppressor and oppressed in order to show the
aberrations of a faulty system. In these plays, which allow
every person to sing, every person is also apt to sin. The
omnific song weaves the whole of an esthetic texture; one
is tempted to surmise that Brecht has likewise shown a per-
manence of corruption in every social class in order to make
of his victims the absolutes of a necessary suffering. The
commoners and the peasants in *The Caucasian Chalk Circle*
are as hard as their repressive masters and as cruel to Grusha;
it is the poor and the destitute who drive Shen-Te to ruin.
The classes meant to be outlined by their struggle become
indistinct because of the emergent figures of individuals.

The Marxian contradiction parallels that of a social play
losing itself within the complexities of the human maze:
both are instances of the dramatic temptation prevailing
over the political. The social flux, central to Brecht's political philosophy, is often the tossing about and the trampling
of human beings (the symbol of which is the battered
wagon of Mother Courage), and it is ultimately the obscure

[7] Translated by H. R. Hays, in *Selected Poems* of Bertolt Brecht,
published by Grove Press, Inc., Copyright © 1947 by Bertolt
Brecht and H. R. Hays.

and fruitless impulses of man himself. In *A Man's a Man,*
the cynical and perceptive Begbick sings a song about man
as a "contradiction." The words are directed at those who
exploit this animal confusion, but the mere statement of
that confusion has a resonance that is profounder than its
intended purpose—it echoes at depths that are beyond all
moral truths and their solutions.

The victims, in this world of turmoil and confusion, turn
unexpectedly to a source of comfort that is as remote from
the tangible assurances of a social program as they themselves are. Although she never complains, Grusha kneels
down and prays in her suffering. Her irrational movement
is not an isolated instance. These people are not figures of
reason, even though a rational voice is heard throughout
condemning a divinity variously allied to more pedestrian
exploiters (for example, in *Saint Joan of the Stockyards;*
or, in *Mahagonny*, the "game-of-God-in-Mahagonny"), or
a Church that refuses political engagement (as in *Señora
Carrar's Rifles*, 1937, which is an episode of the Spanish
Civil War and a topical adaptation of Synge's *Riders to the
Sea*), or one that is as corrupt as its members (in *The Caucasian Chalk Circle*, a character says of a priest, "In Sura
there's one with a real air of sanctity about him, but of
course he charges a fortune." [8]). But even such condemnation is relative in Brecht's mind alongside a more absolute
condemnation: when, for example, he turns his full wrath
on Naziism (*Fear and Misery of the Third Reich*, 1935–
1938), a measure of pity redeems the "poor Jewish god"
Jesus and softens Brecht's irony toward Christians who

[8] *The Caucasian Chalk Circle* appears in *Parables for the Theater,*
two plays by Bertolt Brecht, English version by Eric Bentley and
Maja Apelman, published by Grove Press, Inc., Copyright © 1948
by Eric Bentley.

must, in trembling, hide their Ten Commandments—for these are all victims of a more immediate and more ruthless evil.

Brecht's condemnation never extends to the animal responses of man—he simply notes them as inevitable expressions; there is a bitterness that comes of knowing in many of these choruses (Begbick's commentary, among others). An older wisdom endures in Brecht alongside his scientific optimism and his social consciousness. In the original version of *The Caucasian Chalk Circle*, his singer states with confidence: "You will find [. . .] that the voice of the old poet blends with Soviet tractors." And when a tractor driver asks him whether the play might not be shortened a little, he answers, "No." It is on this dismissal that the story of Grusha starts.

Brecht has sought deep within the human tangle the "contradictions evidenced by the actions and characters of real people" to which the "Organon" refers, and in so doing, he has strayed from the normative ways of logical demonstrations. There comes a moment when the human evidence within the stage person sends the spectator back into himself with too much force: it is then that the spectator sees the person on stage as himself and ascribes his own impulses to that person's gestures. That character is no longer the author's: it lives in the intimate lives of all who *are* that character. Brecht wanted his *Galileo* to represent at least one sort of irresponsibility, in order that the spectator might reject, along with Galileo, a certain point of view:

The crime of Galileo can be considered the "original sin" of modern science. Of the new astronomy, interesting a new class—the bourgeoisie—who looked upon it as a weapon in the social revolution of the times, Galileo made a [pure] science that was strictly circumscribed.[9]

History records that the astronomer was forced to retract his heliocentric theories, first in Tuscany and eventually in Rome before the Inquisition. Brecht says of these disavowals that they "allowed him to pursue his scientific work in a vacuum." [10] In his encounters with the rising class—the bourgeoisie—Galileo is pictured by Brecht as the scientist who refuses engagement (he has written a book on the mechanics of the universe, that is all. Whatever is done or not done with it does not concern him). But when his disciple Sarti attempts to make Galileo take a stand upon the very terms of Brecht's own later commentary, the man Galileo begins to stir within the symbol and frustrates Sarti's efforts. Galileo cannot close his eyes to any objective truth; his is a drama of lucidity, and the founder of experimental physics here subsumes the impartial judges and the performing commentators of the *Lehrstücke*. His passion is scientific research, but it is a passion, that is to say, an intensity and a sensitivity, within the animal being. The clear-sighted critic Galileo notes his own animal presence. That is why Brecht has shown in him not only a hunger for knowledge but also the "avid gluttony" of an old man stuffing himself without a further thought for anything else. The man in Galileo, which is the spectator, comprehends these contradictions; the symbolic figures of social consciousness around Galileo do not. It is little wonder that the "explicitness" of Brecht occasioned so many conflicting interpretations when the play was finally performed in Europe after the war and that French and German critics of the left were able to tax Brecht's own Berliner Ensemble

[9] *Theater der Zeit*, Suppl. 11, 1956.
[10] *Ibid.*

with "dramatizing" the play and, worse, stressing its "tragic focus." [11]

When they grow too independent of the lesson which they are supposed to demonstrate, the people of Brecht distort that lesson—even in the *Lehrstücke*. In the last of these, *The Exception and the Rule*, the purposeful exploiter appears fully cogent, and even courageous, alongside the ineffectiveness of the exploited coolie. The same is very nearly true of the character of Pierpont Mauler, the cynical meat king in Brecht's *Saint Joan*. Conversely, when the villains are too exclusively villainous (the clergy, already shown; the military; the rich; and so on), they seem as caricatures alongside the complex evidence of the principals, and the play rattles because of their mechanical gestures and their emptiness. This evidence is clear to the playwright himself. For example, he is conscious that his adaptation of Gorki's novel, *The Mother*, is too didactic. And the Berliner Ensemble trims a portion of *Señora Carrar's Rifles*, the overly simplistic story of the Spanish mother whose refusal to take sides in the Civil War is overcome.

But when there is blood on the stage, it is the spectator's —since puppets have no blood. *Mother Courage* is the chronicle of a sutler, Anna Fierling, during the religious upheavals of the seventeenth century known as the Thirty Years' War. The suffering of the masses stigmatizes war: Mother Courage loses her children, and her commentary on the events is the minutia to whose monstrous projection the play alludes. But the tough hides of these people show no scars; Mother Courage falters only once, and briefly. When she has lost everything, her very last words are to a departing regiment—"Hey! Take me with you"—and the endless round continues. Few plays of Brecht have been

[11] *Théâtre Populaire*, May 24, 1957.

more disappointing to those seeking a positive message (*Die Neue Zeitung* epitomized this disappointment in 1949: "Brecht merely notes, as a pessimist, and points to the evils of war"). But blood flows in Kattrin, Anna Fierling's daughter. In contrast to her voluble mother, she never speaks. She is dumb—and that dumbness is the first of the marks which the war has left on her. As the war continues, she is also maimed, and eventually she dies because of the war. Symbols can be only themselves; that is why they cannot change. But alongside the figure of Kattrin, the war recedes: she is more important than her dramatic catalyst. When she dies, her reality imparts a single moment of frailness to Anna Fierling, who briefly loses her mind before the body of her daughter. It is only for a moment, however. The point is stressed by the actress Helen Weigel, the co-founder of the Berliner Ensemble, and Brecht's wife, who devised an "exemplary stage gesture" (Brecht's words) for Mother Courage when, seconds later, she gives some coins to the peasants for the burial of her daughter—and then takes one of the coins back. It can be questioned whether this gesture is any more helpful in re-establishing objectivity than is what the "Organon" calls "exemplary music" (written by Hanns Eisler for *Galileo*), music described as triumphant and menacing at once, which foreshadows the revolutionary twist that the lower classes will give to the astronomical theories of the scholar.

Brecht and his disciples have been dissatisfied time and again by the interpretations of these plays by directors, spectators, and critics. Some of the reactions to *Galileo* have been cited. Brecht protested against the Zurich interpretation of *Mother Courage* in the posture of a *mater dolorosa* with the body of her daughter on her knees. The reasons for which *The Threepenny Opera* met with world-

wide acclaim generally dismayed and irritated Brecht: this critique of an opera (the concept is that of Kurt Weill, who composed its music) became an operatic success—and worse. Brecht expected, perhaps as a reaction against its success, a very subtle interpretation of the play. For the "miraculous" saving of MacHeath from the gallows in the final scene, Brecht demanded a real horse and a serious tone when the King's envoy appears on stage bearing the glad tidings, because only such bourgeois regalia can "insure untrammeled pleasure in situations that are per se perfectly unbearable." It is a *"sine qua non* condition of a literature whose condition *sine qua non* is incoherence." This is no small task. The spectator is asked to accept the scenic device as a conventional statement of grandeur so that he may objectify the pleasure he has felt in it and reject it along with the many other implications of falseness in the opera. One wonders whether there does not result a more simple and more immediate form of objectivity from the uneasy laughter of the audience that recognizes the patent falseness of the miraculous outcome and so atones for its sentimental indulgence in this false world of attractive rogues —a world for which one suspects that Brecht himself, and Kurt Weill (no "exemplary music" his), had an asocial weakness. Are not so many of the social symbols old friends in ideological dress—the prostitutes, the Chicago underworld, the petty thugs, and scoundrels of any demimonde?

Is not the idea of "theater" simply one more form of sentimentalism? It can be argued that if the scientific world envisaged by Brecht is able to effect its changes in the relationships of people, in their deepest atavisms, the theater will disappear entirely, along with all other vestiges of a prescientific sentimentalism. But until that happy day, does the theater not exist as an anthropomorphic quantity that defies rational efforts to alter it? It does seem doubtful that as long as theater endures at all, this anthropomorphism will ever allow "mood" (*Stimmung*) to be dissociated from the dramatic performance. One can understand Brecht's desire to resist it in its cheaper forms (satirized as the "moon over Soho" mood in *The Threepenny Opera*), but as mood is "an affectation by emotion," the theater retains it as long as it clings to a human quantity. Brecht may have introduced debatable colloquialisms and stage effects for didactic purposes in his adaptations of Marlowe (*The Life of Edward II of England*) or Schiller (in Brecht's version of *Mary Stuart*, the two contending queens lapse into the idiom of the market place); but when the drunken judge Azdak and the drunken landowner Puntila speak, they have in common a lyric joy in language, and a single dramatic "aura" is created that has little to do with their utterly contrasting symbolism. In the stage play that shows the rising Chicago gangster Ui being coached on stage by an actor of the "unnatural" school which Brecht scorns, the spectators were to have recognized idiosyncrasies of Hitler (the play was not performed during Brecht's lifetime) and laughter would have humanized the "distance" that Brecht wished to preserve as rational anger (and whoever doubts that anger need but read his appended notes to *The Resistible Rise of Arturo Ui*, 1941). Such mockery is Brecht's—but even it can be at times just another one of the character's human foibles.

After his first three, Brecht built every play around a moral postulate and in each he hoped for a political lesson, but as often as not, he entrusted that lesson to the dramatic necessities of the play. In so doing, he became a successor to Pirandello and Cocteau: his plays are often interesting commentaries upon, and analyses of, the dramatic process itself. There is an echo to his plays, a depth which is that of the stage. When that dimension is lost, he is as successful as he wished to be—and as no one else wished: the play becomes intellectual, that is to say, merely parodic; a story is told, or commented upon, or imitated—but the depth of the stage is missing.

Speaking of his craft and beliefs, Brecht said, "One cannot conceive an epic theater lacking in artistry, fantasy, without humor, or the gift of sympathy." Sympathy: the ability to suffer with. How many pages of theory and dogma are subverted by those words? And how far was Brecht, ultimately, from Aristotle, who acknowledged, within a special and very lofty sense, the power of tragedy to teach—anagnorisis?

II ~ EUGÈNE IONESCO:

The Difficulty of Living

I think that it is difficult indeed to breathe and to live;
I think also that it is possible for man not to be a social
creature.

  Eugène Ionesco, "The Heart Is Not Worn on the
Sleeve" (1958)

BIOGRAPHERS of Bertolt Brecht have drawn attention
to his interest in learning. His enjoyment of the intellectual
give and take precedes and informs his love of the theater;
an understanding of his dramatic system compels recognition of this fact. By the time Brecht had committed himself
wholly to the theater, he saw it as a forum for the barter
and testing of ideas. The denudation of the *Lehrstück*
stages represents one of the conclusions of his reasoning:
it is an attempt to strip the stage of that which might distort
his statement or jeopardize its analysis. After 1930, Brecht
accepted the fact that the theater does not allow this sort
of objectivity and that, indeed, it is constantly making an
assertion of its own that does not relate necessarily to the
dramatist's. He apparently realized that in order to attain
the objective climate necessary for an examination of ideas,
there would have to occur first social and psychological
mutations beyond even those which his view of history
allowed—since that view stopped short of rejecting the
residual sentimentalism that is necessary for the stage to
exist at all. Because it was not possible for his writings to
remain objective statements capable of rational control once
they were entrusted to the theater (the body of the stage
and the soul of the spectator), his stage techniques became

devices meant to control the marginal statement of the stage so as to enlist its co-operation or, at least, prevent that statement from subverting his own.

The first plays of Eugène Ionesco show a similar belief in the ability of the playwright to control his dramatic statement even on stage; in the case of the early Ionesco, this belief derives from a simple disregard of the stage. A part of his theory is contained in the subtitle "antiplay" that defines his first stage venture. The petulance of the subtitle also suggests one of Ionesco's antecedents—surrealism, the 1920s' expression of a periodic urge in French letters to assail existing forms. As defined by André Breton, surrealism is the refusal of an individual existence to submit to the posited limitations of existence. This refusal supposes a program of both active destruction and original creation. The destructive aspects of surrealism are inherited from Dada, the systematic subversion of all the forms of a prior acceptance that has become sterile and irritating—be it the social, cultural, or natural function too long unquestioned. Surrealism as a creative force derives from the belief in a human organism capable of transcending, within a dream-world of poetic magic, former limitations. This is not the exploration of a theoretical transcendency or the reliance on a mystique. It represents the modern poetic craving, the desire by the poet to express the unexpressed and the inexpressible, the desire by man to grow beyond himself. This beyond is to be sought within the everyday realm, in the objects, the circumstances, the familiar patterns that are to be "defamiliarized." In practice, the dream and the poetry of surrealism arise out of that which is tangible and prosaic; it is a poetry of objects, its experiments with automatic writing and its cultivated intimacy with madness notwithstanding.

Surrealism achieved a linguistic freedom, a total ellipsis, a liberating concision, a richer and less conscious imagery. It is thus especially in poetry that the movement finds its most valid affirmation. As for its madness, mundane and clinical, its loud iconoclasm, its assault upon the psychic world, these make of it a purveyor of sensationalism whose extravagances have been defined and curtailed by the acceptance of psychoanalysis. The analysis of the fantastic, the cultivation of an oneiric world upon what seems commonplace, the attainment of mutations hitherto unknown are techniques of surrealism which will be found in the drama of Ionesco and which reflect one of the literary influences of his formative years.[1] Ionesco's desire to assault the public may also be due to that influence—unless it be that of Jarry whose *Ubu Roi* (1896) is a high point in invective drama. It should be noted that there has never been any surrealist drama to speak of and that Ionesco himself never belonged to the group. His plays will therefore be analyzed as his own creations without contextual reference.

What must be alluded to first, however, is not the subject matter that equates the concerns of this drama with those of the surrealists, but the point of view—the reaction against a traditional art form before that reaction becomes itself the exemplar of a new form; the moment of destruction that precedes the fact of commitment and stays the destructive impulse. A dramatic pronouncement that proposes an "antiplay" is little different from any other sort of dramatic pronouncement: the last word remains with the stage, which may well redefine even the onslaught directed against it. By Ionesco's own admission, he was not aware of this in 1948 and had yet to evolve from his first "derision" to his

[1] See Edith Mora, "Ionesco: 'Le Rire? L'Aboutissement d'un drame!'" *Nouvelles Littéraires*, Dec. 24, 1959.

eventual "fascination." As a matter of fact, *The Bald So-prano* was not intended for the theater at all. It was merely a nameless bit of fun. Circumstances eventually made Io-nesco a captive of his fun and a playwright. He has described these circumstances a number of times: he was studying English with the aid of "a French-English conversation manual." Language thus distinct from visceral immediacy was nonsense even more acute than it generally is for this linguistically displaced person who sees words as non-assimilable objects (fascinating indeed, and perhaps a little dangerous as are all refractory mysteries)—one of the in-securities to which his drama testifies. It is not that this Rumanian does not know French (the language of his plays). Rather, the opposite is true: he remains *conscious* of it. It is one of the recalcitrant objects in this theater that are chewed but never digested.

Language objectified is amusing, in the manner of any relationship which sudden detachment—short of fear—voids of a former intimacy. "I did not think that this com-edy was a real comedy. In fact, it was only a parody of a play, a comedy comedy. I used to read it to friends, for laughs, when they gathered at my home." Eventually, the manuscript found its way into the hands of a young director, Nicolas Bataille, and it was deemed to be performable. Io-nesco's own title, *English without Tears*, pointed too clearly to the play's origin. The author suggested instead *The English Hour, An Hour of English, Big-Ben Folies* (*sic*). Bataille resisted these suggestions—they misrepresented the play by extending its scope, hinting as they did at satire. By this time Ionesco had run out of ideas. The play re-mained without a title until one of the actors misread a line as "la cantatrice chauve"; in a fitting way, fortuitous cir-cumstances had baptized the play in nonsense.

If Ionesco proposes *The Bald Soprano* merely "for laughs" to the friends for whom he reads it, he is not proposing a play, not even a comic one: he is proposing an experience within actuality. It is not the playwright who is involved in that experience, but the man. Nor is *The Bald Soprano* at that moment even an "antiplay," unless the expression designates something that is not a play, in this particular case a private joke for the benefit of friends. It is only because his action is not completely spontaneous (he *reads* something, he has thus *written* it) that it can be distinguished from any other. The suspicion that *The Bald Soprano* is indeed not a play but merely a private joke remains in the definitive version published by Gallimard in 1954, whose stage directions, the otherwise meaningful but unobtrusive parts of the play, are meant to amuse rather than to enlighten—as are the footnotes in their sense-defying punctiliousness.

The dialogue is mainly in the form of self-contained statements that attempt little interplay. Typically, the play starts as a soliloquy by Mrs. Smith—petty commentaries and platitudes inspired by the meal which the Smiths have just finished. Ensconced in his chair, wearing "English slippers [and] reading an English newspaper, near an English fire," [2] Mr. Smith is drawn into the monologue, at first, only through its insults ("the soup was perhaps a little too salt. It was saltier than you"). When the dialogue *is* initiated, it proceeds in this fashion:

[2] *The Bald Soprano* appears in *Four Plays* by Eugène Ionesco, translated by Donald M. Allen, published by Grove Press, Inc., Copyright © 1958 by Grove Press, Inc. (A shortened version of the translation of *The Bald Soprano* was published in New World Writing, Ninth Mentor Selection: © 1956 by Eugène Ionesco.) Other quotations from this translation are on succeeding pages.

MR. SMITH (*still reading his paper*): Tsk, it says here that
    Bobby Watson died.
MRS. SMITH: My God, the poor man! When did he die?
MR. SMITH: Why do you pretend to be astonished? You
    know very well that he's been dead these past
    two years. Surely you remember that we at-
    tended his funeral a year and a half ago.
MRS. SMITH: Oh yes, of course I do remember. I remem-
    bered it right away, but I don't understand why
    you yourself were so surprised to see it in the
    paper.
MR. SMITH: It wasn't in the paper. It's been three years
    since his death was announced. I remembered it
    through an association of ideas.
MRS. SMITH: What a pity! He was so well preserved.

Such conversation is little more than co-operation in
sense destruction. Its meaninglessness is echoed by a clock
that has been chiming erratically since curtain rise. Other
mechanical presences are introduced and remain similarly
isolated and static. They elicit no surprise, no reaction of
any sort in the other characters; they do not make any
distinctive statement. The Martins are introduced by the
maid, and the dialogue of this new couple grows out of their
mutual wonder over the coincidences of their parallel exist-
ences. This process is the reverse of the incongruity that
fails to surprise; here it is the expected that evokes stereo-
typed amazement. The Smiths then join the Martins, and
the exercise in sense destruction becomes choral, with the
addition of a fireman (who belongs to the same incongruous
race as the erratic clock). Eventually, the play attains a
verbal frenzy of sense-voided sounds. The lights go out.
When they come on again, the first lines of the opening
scene are repeated, this time by Mrs. Martin. No single

ending, however, impressed itself with compelling force-fulness on the author, who has indicated a number of vari-ants upon which he looks with similarly benign indifference or spurious favor.

One of those whose soul-steeling task it has been to turn Ionesco into English, Donald Watson, has grouped the play-wright's linguistic "styles" under the following headings: "banality, exaggeration (to include repetition and incon-sequence), illogicality, distortion and elevation." The first of these, and perhaps the last, mocks that which is trivial in daily life through pedestrian and unrelenting parody. The opening monologue of Mrs. Smith is an example of this technique. The other headings subsume instances of lan-guage losing even subliminal meaning. Whereas banality and linguistic emphasis used for disparagement point to the paucity of meaning, the other devices assert the demise of intellectual control.

The subversion of reason may be partial or absolute. Nonsense may acknowledge rational norms by simply over-turning them. (In the conversation between Mr. and Mrs. Smith, this sort of fun is sought in two ways: 1, through improbability—"He's been dead these past two years. Surely you remember that we attended his funeral a year and a half ago"; 2, through an inversion of the logical prop-osition—"He's been dead these past two years. [. . .] It's been three years since his death was announced.") Or again, nonsense may develop in pure form, without even the acknowledgment of an external reason. Donald Watson recalls asking Ionesco what the point was of certain puz-zling passages in *Amédée* (1953) and receiving the answer: "None at all, that *is* the point. Put anything you like." Such removal from reason can come about through the degenerative process of talk, as meaning (which is at best tenuous) gradually evaporates with the disappearance of intellective links. Words may also be voided of intelligence through statements made simultaneously by people speaking at cross-purposes because of the confrontation of mutually closed worlds. Words may further lose their meaning in a contest with mechanical sounds that eventually dehumanize the much frailer words. In yet another flight to madness, any device that shows words to be only part sense by emphasizing that they are also part sound—the pun, alliterative rhythm, word coining—may swing over entirely to sound, as happens at the climax of *The Bald Soprano*.

The subversion of sense is accompanied, in its benign stage, by the irrelevant assertion of mechanical objects, such as the erratic clock in the Smiths' living room or the unlikely fireman ("of course in uniform and [. . .] wearing an enormous shining helmet"). They are merely incongruous, but their incongruity exists only to the extent that it acknowledges, in another world, clocks that chime on the hour and firemen that come in response to fire alarms. When, however, the dehumanization of speech inhibits its human source, it opens the stage to more sinister objects, those antihuman forces that have been growing steadily on the periphery of the human being, like the ever-enlarging corpse that eventually breaks into the set of *Amédée* and collapses it, the deluge of eggs that brings to a close *The Future Is in Eggs* (1951), or the uninterrupted flow of furniture that ends by clogging up completely the apartment in *The New Tenant* (1953).

It was inevitable that sooner or later the plays of Ionesco, written as they were in the years following the Second World War, would become associated with the *absurd*, a postwar climate wherein a number of French authors thrived. Although neither the concept of the absurd nor its formulation was new at the time, not even to French letters, the notion became topical largely because of an "essay on the absurd" by Albert Camus, *The Myth of Sisyphus* (first published in 1942), which proposed "a description, in pure form, of an illness of the spirit." In bald terms, the essay is an examination of certain consequences that follow from the premise that a gap which is permanent and cannot be bridged separates self from surroundings. The book is not a speculative treatise but the description of a personal experience—"a sensibility of the absurd [. . .] not a philosophy of the absurd"—since, basically, it suggests that reality and experience are irremediably separate.

The absurd is first something which is *felt*, an awareness of the disparity in man between his dream and his demarcation. The fundamental peculiarity of the human urge is its infinite extension; the fundamental peculiarity of being is necessary limitation. Awareness of this discrepancy comes from a sense of ill-being and frustration due to the senselessness of life as it is lived daily, the futility implicit in its transitoriness within the unending flow of time, the impossibility of contact beyond the self. At every level, man finds himself hemmed in by his body. He cannot follow his aspiration beyond it, he cannot project his consciousness into the physical world around him; things remain hopelessly and forever objectified—and a like "thingness" informs even other human beings:

If I were a tree amidst trees, a cat amidst animals, this life would have a meaning or, better, this problem would be meaningless for I would be a part of this world. I would *be* this world against which I now stand because of my full consciousness and the familiarity which I crave. This pathetic reason is that which sets me against all creation.[3]

The mind may be called on to react against the "evidence of the senses," but it fails. The best that it has achieved has been to inscribe labels between itself and chaos:

And here are trees and I know their coarse texture, water and I experience its taste. Amidst these scents of grass and the stars, at night, how shall I deny, eventides when the heart relaxes, this world whose power and whose drives I feel? Yet all the science in the world will be helpless to assure me that this world belongs to me. You describe it to me and you teach me how to classify it. You enumerate its laws and in my thirst for knowledge I admit that they are true. You disassemble its works and my hope increases. In the final account, you tell me that this fascinating and many-colored universe is reducible to atoms and that the atom itself can be reduced to the electron. All this is fine and I am waiting for you to continue. But you speak to me of an invisible planetary system where electrons gravitate around a nucleus. You explain this world to me through an image. I recognize then that you have been reduced to poetry: I shall never know.

Traditionally, the way out of this dilemma has been the acceptance of some transcendental reference, an absolute such as Truth or God. Since the mind cannot grasp absolutes short of private revelation, reliance upon them must be an act of faith. Camus cannot accept this "leap" which sensory evidence mocks and which can at best mask, but never dispel, the sensory evidence. The dilemma remaining insoluble, there is another way out, suicide. But suicide too is rejected by Camus, since, in the same way as the "leap of

[3] Quotations from *The Myth of Sisyphus* by Albert Camus are made with the kind consent of its American publishers, Alfred A. Knopf, Inc.

faith" ("philosophical suicide"), it is an irrational flight with no more justification than any other effort to transcend the nontranscendable absurd.

It is upon these rejections of faith and suicide alike that Camus develops his ethical statement. Suicide and faith are attempts to destroy the consciousness which man has of the absurd and, therefore, acknowledgments of it. But they are also the evidence of an inner voice that protests relentlessly against the absurd. Since even gestures of submission cannot exorcise the stark fact of his being, man's only sense of purpose abides in his instinctive revulsion against his nonsensical fate: he is able to assert himself only to the extent of his *revolt*. The only positive statement of which man is capable is thus tied to the absurd. His single assertion deriving from the intensity of his revolt, man must recognize his absurd condition to the utmost of his lucidity so as to keep alive in him the heightened consciousness of his refusal. He is then able to endure in the knowledge of his hopelessness while rendering meaningful through his awareness his every moment of sentience.

The first notes for what was to be *The Myth of Sisyphus* were jotted down by Camus in 1938; his first full statement on the subject came that same year in the form of a play, *Caligula,* the theater having always been a congenial mode for Camus. The play relates the facts about the Roman emperor as they were collected by Suetonius (*The Lives of the Caesars,* Book IV), whom Camus considers to be a reliable reporter. The Caligula of Suetonius is at first a youth given to dissimulation, histrionics, and a morbid interest in cruelty. But, in part thanks to his ability to dissimulate, he is, at the death of Tiberius, "the prince most earnestly desired by the great part of the provincials and soldiers [. . .], as well as by the whole body of the city populace."

In the first part of his reign, Caligula takes steps to render the operation of government more efficient and humane and to make the population saner in its moral habits and happier. This first period, covering a span of eight months, deals with "Caligula as emperor." The second tells "of his career as a monster."

Presumably because of the power vested in him, the emperor's megalomania became progressively more evident in his actions. He appeared at times in the garb of various divinities, including that of Venus; he invited the moon to share his bed with him; he treated his favorite sister Drusilla as his lawful wife and heir to the throne, even though—to compound this madness—she was a married woman at the time. To such acts of megalomania as concerned only his own person, he added a greater number that took into account the relation of others to him: these acts are marked by Caligula's unrelenting sadism. It is noteworthy that the indiscriminate listing of Suetonius makes these acts appear to be frequently, though not necessarily, the anguished reality of what would have been innocuous as merely small talk. As reported by Suetonius, the cruelty of Caligula is informed by a sense of logic (close to irony) that demands the *realization* of ideas. He deplored at one time that his reign had not been marked by public disasters to make it famous; he thought of destroying the poems of Homer, asking why he should not have the same privilege as Plato, who excluded Homer from his Republic. A man who offered his life for the recovery of the emperor, but who considered the vow rhetorical after the emperor was well again, Caligula had decked with sacred boughs and finally killed.

Being a statement of the absurd, Camus' play is concerned only with the second part of Suetonius' account, the history of Caligula as monster. The death of Drusilla marks the change in the once "perfect emperor." It is not his pain over the loss of Drusilla that accounts for his change, since the play states clearly that his reason is not affected; his very first words are spoken with naturalness and before any evidence of insanity—"I am not mad." In order to make an ethical prolegomenon to the erratic acts of the man described by Suetonius, Camus stresses their sardonic coherence. Rather than a madman, Caligula is a man whose mind cannot take in the death of the woman for whom he felt a love beyond the power of convention and laws to alter. The death of Drusilla is Caligula's inoculation by the absurd: from now on, he is a man *aware*. The first positive statement of the absurd Caligula is his lucidity.

The evidence that overwhelms the hero has two immediate consequences. He becomes a demonstrator of the absurd and its precipitant; but he is also that which is precipitated. The avowal of his consciously absurd life forces all others to live in the same absurd climate. Like the emperor of Suetonius, he voices dissatisfaction with a reign lacking the plague that would render its votaries significant, but he goes beyond his prototype in asserting, "It is I who replace the plague"; thereafter, no hiding place remains. In refusing to recognize the usual disguises, Caligula forces those around him to declare their individual truth; each is constrained to make the statement that displays a human being wholly naked. In one of the play's lighter moments, the glib patrician finds that words no longer make the man, that you do not offer life as idly as you wish health. In more serious moments, Caligula's closest friends, Cherea, Scipion, and Caesonia, must declare what they are when friendship has become as meaningless as the rest.

But Caligula is not merely an instrument: his every fiber

is tensed against the ridiculous lot of man. This supposed madman fights down his emotions when he says, "Men die and they are not happy"; and his tears are genuine as he comments, "Men cry because things are not what they should be." But these are passing moments of weakness. He refuses to allow his awareness to bind him; his strength derives from the assertion of his refusal and condemns by contrast those who are not as consequent or courageous: "I must have the moon, or happiness, or immortality—something that is mad perhaps, but not of this world." If he becomes Venus or the moon's lover, it is not only in order to show how illusory are the desires of man, but also in order to assert the full force and the validity of those desires. Tensed as he is between the absolutes of his desire and his doom, his vibrancy sounds the single note of which men are capable. It is this existence-signifying awareness that illuminates for Camus the moment when Caligula is stabbed—who, "as he lay upon the ground and with writhing limbs called out that he still lived." The last words spoken in Camus' play, "Je suis encore vivant!" are the unyielding summation of the hero: he and his assertion are forever one.

Another view of man's senseless lot gained currency in the years just after the Second World War—that of Jean-Paul Sartre. It internalizes the duality from which Camus derives his view of the absurd. Sartre sees the unsatisfactory confrontation of man and the world into which he is willed as an unacceptably contingent statement, even though Camus posits both principles of the antinomy as indemonstrable facts. For Satre, the absurd is not what he terms Camus' disparity between "man's rational demands and the irrationality of the world." Rather, it is inherent in the positing of existence—a datum that has no justification and that will not allow even the form of a dialogue in which the absurd

monologue of Camus presents itself. Since there is no binomial in this assertion, the absurd of Sartre is not evident in
colloquy; until an ethical statement is attempted, his absurd
discloses merely a condition of existence. It is most likely
for this reason that the plays of Sartre cannot concern themselves centrally with the absurd, but show instead such
ethical action as is possible within the absurd climate. However, a full description of that climate does occur in a novel.
Nausea (1938) purports to be the diary of Antoine Roquentin's dreary days spent in a provincial town in fruitless
pursuit of some historical research. His first intimation of
the absurd is so violent that it impels him to record his experience: he has become uncomfortably aware of the
"thingness" of a pebble which he was about to skim over
the water. Not, however, until a number of other experiences have accrued around this one will he be able to give
a name to the expanding circle of his awareness. His epiphany comes with an acute and sudden feeling of *detachment*
which he experiences before the roots of a chestnut tree in
a public park:

The word absurdity is coming to life under my pen; a little
while ago, in the garden, I couldn't find it, but neither was I
looking for it, I didn't need it: I thought without words, *on*
things, *with* things. Absurdity was not an idea in my head, or
the sound of a voice, only this long serpent dead at my feet,
this wooden serpent. Serpent or claw or root or vulture's
talon, what difference does it make. And without formulating
anything clearly, I understood that I had found the key to
Existence, the key to my Nauseas, to my own life. In fact, all
that I could grasp beyond that returns to this fundamental
absurdity. Absurdity: another word; I struggle against words;
down there I touched the thing.[4]

[4] Jean-Paul Sartre, *Nausea*. All rights reserved. Reprinted by
permission of New Directions, Publishers.

And, anticipating the formulation and the content of *Caligula*, Roquentin comments:

A movement, an event in the tiny coloured world of men is only relatively absurd: by relation to the accompanying circumstances. A madman's ravings, for example, are absurd in relation to the situation in which he finds himself, but not in relation to his delirium. But a little while ago I made an experiment with the absolute or the absurd. This root—there was nothing in relation to which it was not absurd.[5]

Sartrian man can make only such statements as dispel the notion of any absurd that is less than the absurd over which he has no hold and within which his every statement is contained (and perhaps Roquentin's diary is his only salvation—the creation through the work of art of a limited, personal order within chaos). But that which he is able to explain within the absolute absurd can effect no linkage with it. Therefore, it is not possible for Sartre to make of his book an instance of the absurd, a container instead of the thing contained. He can only propose a man sufficiently like the reader who, it is hoped, will endow the character with "the gift of his entire being, with his passions, his prejudices, his sympathies, his sexual temperament, his scale of values" (Sartre, in *What Is Literature?*). If the author is able to attract the reader in this way, it will then be possible for that reader to attain, with Roquentin, the experience of the absolute absurd.

For the same reason, it is necessary to accept the full sorrow of Caligula's "How hard, how bitter it is to become a man!" Unless Caligula is conscious of the depths of human suffering, he can be aware of the absurd only academically.

[5] *Ibid.* Hereafter, *absurd* as noun or adjective will have the meaning given to it by either Camus or Sartre.

Therefore Caligula remains a *man* on stage, and a particularized person—an emperor, a man in Roman dress. He must assume more human reality than does the Caligula of Suetonius in part two, that part in which the historian collects documentary evidence for the portrayal of an antiman, Caligula "as a monster." If it were possible for a playwright to represent a character wholly demented, that character would be a stage figure alienated from a spectator who is unable to assimilate his gestures, and that dispassionate spectator would have to accept him as being "absurd in relation to the situation in which he finds himself"—that is to say, as a real, but circumscribed, manifestation on stage of the absurd, within the reference of the spectator's reality. As Sartre indicates, this would be tantamount to making within limits a statement of what both authors accept as an absolute and, hence, an unsatisfactory solution, especially as the dramatic event would be representing itself as a genuine instance of the absurd. But the very essence of the dramatic performance shows that a wholly demented figure cannot be created.

Inasmuch as the theater was never "invented," it is not possible to "disinvent" it. It has grown out of unformulated needs, and the shape in which it endures institutionally (the institution having prevailed over the need) is expressive of the human relationships which it implies. Because its formal aspects—the institution—have grown in proportion as they restricted and disciplined the human impulse, there has been a tendency to "think" about the theater and to manipulate ("experimentally") certain parts of it. Such manipulation is limited, on the one hand, by the human intangibles that underlie the dramatic process and, on the other, by the impossibility of the experimenter's changing the outward shape of the anthropomorphic theater without regard to its human identity since, divorced from that human identity, its structure has no meaning.

For Camus to make of Caligula a madman would have meant to choose opposition to this human identity and to provoke an instinctive reflex in the spectator, an attempt to give cohesion to the personality of the character by establishing his consonance "in relation to his delirium." As the theater lures its spectator only with live bait, the spectator who is faced with a stage figure whose irrationality is an obstacle to his comprehension will try to reconcile the fragmented parts of a human being—the presence of the actor providing a continuing temptation for him to do so. Since madness cannot be an absolute, it is possible that through any lesser perversion of rationality the spectator would have arrived at *a* Caligula through his aberrations, explaining the man in terms of those aberrations without necessarily accepting his aberrant actions. Camus was not willing to risk this; therefore, Caligula is not mad: he remains, like Roquentin, a man fully visible, one whom the spectator may well become so that, if such possession is effected, Caligula's desperate gestures will be accomplished in the anxiety of the spectator.

The history of Ionesco the playwright is the account of a losing battle against the human sympathy of the stage. There is a human being on stage prior to the moment when the laughter of the spectator signifies that this human being has ceased to exist—has become an object. Such momentary reductions are conceivable; but a theater made wholly of objects is merely a contradiction in terms, and implicit in the nonreconciliation of those terms is the demise of a stage purporting to be a genuine sample of the absurd. It is in this sense that Sartre is able to say, "Nothing which exists can be comic."

Ionesco's laughter has disturbed the theorists intent on making of his theater a cross section of the absurd. The implications of his laughter are several. At the level of pun or alliteration, his language is a parlor game into which the spectator enters with no particular trepidation; within the artificial but urbane limits of the play, the spectator expects to assert effortless control and achieves it in effortless laughter. Conceived as just such a game, *The Bald Soprano* seldom moves beyond the limits of harmless banter, even on stage, and sets the pattern for similar moments that occur in all subsequent plays of Ionesco. But if this sort of mental tomfoolery is pursued further, to the point where communication is in doubt, the consequences of the game are changed. If the change from sense to nonsense is unpremeditated, the spectator may be startled: the parlor play is interrupted, reality intrudes. The intrusion is short-lived. Surprise exists only as a sudden departure from that which is familiar; if it is extended or repeated, familiarity returns. If, for example, the audience cannot give more meaning to senseless words than can those who mouth them, the audience detaches itself from what may have been a momentary assertion of reality (surprise at the senseless words) but has since died in mechanical repetition. At the moment of this death, the play achieves its only valid claim to absurdity by losing its frame of reference—the spectator.

In seeking more than merely incipient moments of absurd perception, the author tries to find a more lasting way to affect the spectator than merely through surprise. In nearly every play of Ionesco, someone laments the failure of language: Bérenger, as he pleads with a sense-void assassin at

the close of *The Unhired Killer* [6] (1957); the deaf-mute
Orator struggling to express himself before the final curtain
of *The Chairs* (1951); Ionesco himself, as he attempts to
communicate with his critics in *The Alma Impromptu* [7]
(1955)—the dramatic impromptu (formal in manner and
carefully written) having become since Molière, or Giraudoux, a way for French dramatists to express their views on
the theater. In cases such as these, the failure of language
hurts someone. Laughter is stilled, the lament supposes a
human being, and the play is returned to the human reality
of the spectator.

Laughter in the theater (as elsewhere) is short-lived. It
lasts long enough for a human being to die, not long enough
for him to stay dead. For the spectator cannot long remain
alone while the gift of himself goes abegging; he must resur-
rect his victim, if only to have the human food upon which
his next outburst of laughter depends. Those who have
tried to square Ionesco's laughter with the idea of a nonhuman theater have suggested that the spectator accepts
Ionesco's stage as a representational segment of the absurd
—at which, of course, he cannot laugh. Instead, he recognizes himself in the absurd world of the stage and effects,
in laughter, the release of his frustrations. This ingenious
explanation supposes a spectator no less ingenious: one who
is able to find himself on the absurd stage (thus a stage

[6] Translated as *The Killer*, which appears in *The Killer and
Other Plays* by Eugène Ionesco, translated by Donald Watson,
published by Grove Press, Inc., Copyright © by John Calder
(Publishers) Ltd. 1960. Quotations in subsequent pages are from
this translation.

[7] Translated as *Improvisation, or The Shepherd's Chameleon*,
which appears in *The Killer and Other Plays* by Eugène Ionesco,
translated by Donald Watson, published by Grove Press, Inc.,
Copyright © by John Calder (Publishers) Ltd. 1960. A quotation
on p. 75 from this translation.

which, although it is absurd, is nevertheless not alienated from him) while at the same time he feels superior to it. In addition to the contradiction which such self-disparagement-for-release implies, it supposes a view of the absurd demeaned to the conventional levels of comedy and a far cry from the oppressive absolute of Camus or Sartre.

It has been noted that the close of *The Bald Soprano* repeats the words and gestures of the opening but with new faces. In the same play, one of the many misunderstandings between Mr. and Mrs. Smith develops over the identity of Bobby Watson:

MR. SMITH: Poor Bobby, he'd been dead for four years and he was still warm. A veritable living corpse. And how cheerful he was!
MRS. SMITH: Poor Bobby.
MR. SMITH: Which poor Bobby do you mean?
MRS. SMITH: It is his wife that I mean. She is called Bobby too, Bobby Watson. Since they both had the same name, you could never tell one from the other when you saw them together.

The interchangeability of people and their proliferation are favorite tricks of Ionesco. *The Lesson* (1950) proposes an action that re-echoes indefinitely: it starts and ends with the front doorbell that announces the arrival of a student, so that the final curtain leaves the spectator with the assumption that another victim will once again fall into the hands of the homicidal teacher, as have already the forty others to whom the play refers. In *The Alma Impromptu*, the critic who first appears on stage is Bartholomeus. Then, as he asks the character called Ionesco to read the play which he is in the act of writing, and which is in fact the play being performed by them, there enters necessarily a Bartholomeus II, and thereafter a Bartholomeus III. In

Jacques, or Submission [8] (1950), a whole family of Jacqueses springs up, and out of Roberte I, Jacques' fiancée, a Roberte II, and so on. Ionesco, when he denies the presence of conventional "characters" on his stage, points to this interchangeability. [9] This has been interpreted as a negation of human personality by critics who believe that Ionesco's stage figures are not subject to conventional appropriation by the spectator.

It should be noted at the outset that not all such duplications or multiplications are of the same kind. The one conjured up briefly by the Smiths grows out of the same linguistic nonsense that allows a corpse four years dead to be still warm in order to play on the words "living corpse." The doorbell that rings at the start and the close of *The Lesson* is redundancy of a different sort. Here, a movement which had been brought to completion is initiated again; attention is not drawn to the personality of the characters involved but rather to the inexorable movement in which they are caught.

In the case of the actual multiplication of stage figures, yet another operation is involved. The multiplication of Bartholomeuses is an expressionistic stage device, the physical proliferation of speculative possibilities. Bartholomeus, in his simultaneous incarnations, is a morality figure representing the playwright's taunts. It is inane to speak of the deprivation of personality in a morality figure, since it is not a *person;* and yet it is only such figures that are "interchangeable" in Ionesco's theater. They are the ones that perform their *danse macabre* around the hero, a dance into

---

[8] Translated as *Jack, or The Submission,* which appears in *Four Plays* by Eugène Ionesco, translated by Donald M. Allen, published by Grove Press, Inc., Copyright © 1958 by Grove Press, Inc. A quotation on p. 76 is from this translation.

[9] For example, in the French weekly *Arts,* Aug. 14–20, 1953.

which the hero does not join because he is of a different sort: he is substance, they are symbol. In *The Alma Impromptu,* the playwright never loses his human coefficient; the family of homonyms that springs up around Jacques, intent on effecting his submission, never affects Jacques himself. The proliferation of these figures around the protagonist is kindred to the proliferation of objects: they are a menace whose reality is evidenced only by the human being whom they endanger. They are depersonalized indeed —since they belong to the classification object—but they are so only in order to establish the evidence of the life to which they are a threat.[10]

Instead of a theater whose nonrationality is supposed to be a statement of the absurd, Ionesco has contrived a drama of anxiety. Nonsense that is sufficiently epic becomes the damnation of the human being who persists on stage and whose definition is a counterstatement to the absurd.

As might be expected in a theater so consistently derived from the confrontation with language, there exists in Io-

[10] Duplication that does not depersonalize is of course of a different sort again. It is conceivable that the human victim might join in the macabre round of his tormentors (the old people in *The Chairs* and Amédée depart quite content, as if they had been fooled). At such a moment, the eradication of a human being points to the human being that was; the human being does not turn object because he is engulfed by objects. In *Victims of Duty* (1952), a policeman asks Choubert to "descend" into his past in search of a missing person. In so doing, Choubert assumes aspects of his former self, while his wife and the policeman turn into figures associated with those former states. In this case, it is the symbol that is redeemed by the person as the mechanical tormentors of the protagonist temporarily share in his reality. Similarly, in *Amédée, or How to Get Rid of It,* a former Amédée and his wife are conjured up by the protagonist. These are conventional stage devices that do no more damage to the reality of the person than do, in Proust, the successive incarnations of Mme Verdurin, the baron de Charlus, or Odette de Crécy.

nesco even that play on words that illuminates the human dilemma of his people. The drama of his that comes closest to achieving a satisfactory balance between the irreality that menaces the human presence and the assertion of that presence is *The Unhired Killer*. The human assertion here is that of Bérenger, one of the names that designate Ionesco's "little man." In a nameless city, an architect has conceived and built a "radiant" inner city where the grass is greener, the skies are bluer, and the sun shines more brightly. But it is being turned into a ghost town by a maniacal killer who lures his victims to their doom through a weird bit of nonsense: he offers to show them "the colonel's snapshot." By means of this bait, he is able to draw them close to one of the ponds that ornament the radiant city, and he drowns them. Bérenger is obsessed by the senseless repetition of the homicidal gesture (another pattern of mechanical repetition that evinces a malevolent fate), and he is sucked into the orbit of the killer, causing the architect (the voice of indifferent reason) to remark, "The victims are so determined to revisit the scene of the crime!"

Ionesco's is a drama of such victims. It is not with anti-characters that these plays are concerned; each play centers on the most ordinary of people in the process of being destroyed (but, as in tragedy, never destroyed before the final curtain: there remains throughout the play, and centrally, a person). It is the agent of this destruction that is the anti-character. Critics have mistakenly made of this agency the protagonist, presumably because of the real protagonist's insignificance. In reality, however, Ionesco has not done away with psychological drama of a conventional sort beyond replacing the dialogue of that drama by monologue (and this, again, is the way of tragedy, for unless the play is of the "detective story" variety derided by the author in *Victims of Duty*, the cards are stacked against the hero from the start).

The anticharacter, whether or not it is an object, is the evidence of a steadily growing and evil strength. In the "naturalistic" plays of Ionesco, this force is represented by the objects that dominate and fill the stage as the curtain falls—the furniture in *The New Tenant*, the eggs of *The Future Is in Eggs*, the endlessly long corpse of the love that once was between the principals of *Amédée* (and, for good measure, the giant mushrooms that add to the demented flora of that play). There are also episodic sprees of the same sort within the plays, such as the multiplying coffee cups in *Victims of Duty* and the rash of brief cases in *The Unhired Killer*. Matter is rampant, a private fixation of the author: "Matter fills everything, takes up all space, stifles under its mass all freedom." [11] He thus recommends that "the props have a part, the objects breathe, the sets come to life, the symbols become tangible." [12]

Because these objects—eggs, furniture, brief cases—are familiar, they do not adumbrate satisfactorily the irrational, but divert the attention of the spectator to the simple incongruity of their proliferation, a misdirection encouraged by the fun poking that subverts so much of these plays.

Entrapment of a more convincing sort comes through the monsters that are implicit in this conventional world (every play of Ionesco is set, at some time or in its totality, in an average middle-class living room). The most apparent of these is ugliness, for which Ionesco's dramas show a veritable partiality, even when there is no good reason for it. The very first picture of the playwright Ionesco in *The*

---

[11] "Le Point de départ," in *Cahiers des Quatre Saisons*, Aug. 1955.
[12] "Expérience du théâtre," in *La Nouvelle Nouvelle Revue Française*, Feb. 1958.

Alma Impromptu (deleted in translation) shows him with his head on his manuscripts, snoring, and holding a ball-point pen "with the tip upward." Even noise is repetitively ugly (in *The Unhired Killer*, the French stage directions refer to it as an "uglification"). There are repeated appearances of disgusting old people (in *The Chairs*, *Jacques*, and *The Unhired Killer*, for example); strange genetic mutations affect even the principals (Jacques has green hair); and there are outright monsters—limbs are unaccountably withered (Edouard, in *The Unhired Killer*), women sport additional noses and fingers (Roberte II, in *Jacques*), people grow hides, and horns and change into Pachydermata (*Rhinoceros*, [13] 1958).

Such is the prehensile world, dank and stifling, in which the monsters luxuriate. But their ultimate strength lies in their ability to devolop just as well within the vitals of any human being. The spectator recognizes them more readily in the depths of his own experience than he does in the unexpected treachery of innocent objects. In "Expérience du théâtre," Ionesco speaks of such intimate knowledge and

---

[13] *Rhinoceros and Other Plays* by Eugène Ionesco, translated by Derek Prouse, published by Grove Press, Inc., Copyright © by John Calder (Publishers) Ltd. 1960.

Anti-*physis* symbolized by physical deformation is a device at least as old as the metamorphosis of Lucifer; melodrama never relinquished it. But the French stage in the second half of the twentieth century has been especially liberal and explicit in materializing the horrible symbol of the nonhuman or of the dehumanized person. In addition to the rhinoplastic ladies and the rhinocerical men of Ionesco, there come to mind the crabs and mollusks of Sartre (*The Prisoners of Altona*); a rubbery horror in *The Empire Builders*, by Boris Vian, called a *Schmürz*; the character of Arthur Adamov who loses his limbs on stage, one by one, in *The Long and Short of Maneuvering*; the emperor who puts his on display in *The Buffalo-Toad* by Armand Gatti; those who lose theirs in Samuel Beckett's garbage cans (*Endgame*); etc.

recommends it as a starting point for drama. The playwright's task is to "bring forth anxieties, inner ghosts"—
a repeated concern of Ionesco, who voices it more explicitly,
with the statement of its Aristotelian universality, in *The
Alma Impromptu:*

> For me, the theatre is the projection onto the stage of the
> world within: it is in my dreams, my anguish, my dark desires,
> my inner contradictions that I reserve the right to find the
> stuff of my plays. [It is] a part of the heritage of my ancestors,
> a very ancient deposit to which all mankind may lay claim.

The only distinction of Ionesco's protagonist comes from
his sensitivity to such anxieties and inner ghosts. Otherwise,
he is the utterly colorless "little man," settled in the most
ordinary of petty bourgeois surroundings, naïve in his beliefs, and limited in his ethical concerns to conventional do-
goodism. Primary forces in subverting his world are the
skeletons which the bourgeois are normally able to keep in
their closets. *His* inevitably escape, in conformity with the
kinetic laws that impel all evil manifestations on this stage.

Since any overenlargement of normal processes is a threat,
lethal gigantism can develop from the very criteria of normalcy. Such a criterion is sexuality, which here subjugates
what it normally informs. It renders grotesque the posturing
of middle-aged bourgeois wives (in *Amédée* or in *Victims
of Duty*), senescent and ugly people (in *The Chairs*), and
even figures of respectability. (In *The Lesson*, for example,
the frenetic climax between student and teacher ends in the
assassination of the student by the teacher; but in the lasciv-
iousness of the girl, their increasingly erotic exchanges, the
merely symbolic knife with which the murder is performed,
their respective positions during the act, Ionesco has made
it clear that this is in fact a rape. Like all the other overgrown forces, sexuality kills in this drama.) The libido as

monster twice confirms the human essence of the character
at whose expense it has grown: once in the destruction
which it is able to work only on living flesh, a second time
in asserting the kinship of the spectator who is bound to
the character's shame. In describing the climactic embrace
of Jacques and Roberte II and the erotic ballet which their
families dance around them, the stage directions of *Jacques*
specify that the scene should "produce in the audience a
feeling of embarrassment, awkwardness, and shame." Mon-
strously overgrown, the spermatic act adds to the viscidness
in which a human being is drowning.

Frustration is another form which the erosion of human
personality can take. Not only are the protagonists unable
to cope with the external assertions of evil, but they also
can offer no resistance to it within themselves. Bérenger
(in *The Unhired Killer*) resorts to action against the maniacal assassin. First to come in his path are the stupid and
huge objects, enormous policemen, that tower over him and
assert their senseless authority through the guilt with which
their presence fills the one who approaches them. After an
agonizing delay, for daylight is dwindling (the sun, merely
referred to in these plays, is an expression of regret for life
as it might have been), Bérenger starts again on his way to
the prefecture. Ironically, this is an ally which, even if he
were able to reach it, could offer him at best only more
policemen. But the fact is that he cannot reach it, and the
words of his assertion that turn into meaningless sound even
as he speaks them are for once a felicitously dramatic statement of his impotence (not rendered in the English translation): "I love the human race, but at a distance. What's
that matter, when I'm interested in the fate of mankind?
Fact is that I'm acting . . . (*He smiles.*) I'm acting . . .

I macting . . . Imacting . . . difficult to pronounce!"
When the killer steps into his path, he exhausts every
rational argument, but words—since there is nothing else
—will fail him again.

Frustration, like sexuality, is a part of the human predicament. Although both develop on this stage at the expense
of the creature which they were supposed to define, they
remain nevertheless aspects of that definition. In *The Alma
Impromptu,* Ionesco makes use of a playwright called Ionesco to show the extent of human frustration; the character who wrestles with his tormentors on stage while living the play which he is writing is in fact Ionesco writing
The Alma Impromptu. At his most successful, Ionesco is
able to hint at the noncontingency of these states of being
and succeeds in making them seem necessary. At such moments, his play becomes epic: there is a glimpse of the human
being alone, performing a meaningless gesture that expresses
his unbounded vision and his ridiculously short reach. Such
is the hopeless monologue of Bérenger before the killer. The
individual's hope and his very gesture die echoless—in the
muffling viscidness of a dreamworld to which he can give
no direction, no dimension. In *The Chairs,* the proliferation
of objects is stilled. The many empty chairs which the old
man and the old woman have placed on the stage will not
multiply. What will multiply is their illusion as they people
the chairs with the regalia of their vision. For once, it is the
overaccumulation of nothingness that brings the principals
to their doom. At the end, after they have drowned in this
void, the Orator steps forth to make his statement but, in
this oneiric world, he is a deaf-mute and only meaningless
sounds issue from his throat. In desperation, he grabs a piece
of chalk and tries to write his message on a blackboard. The

dream cannot be rent, however, and his hand is able to trace only the incomplete letters and the meaningless sounds of his atrophied vocal cords.

When Bérenger hastens to the prefecture on a treadmill of helplessness, the play marks time between the statements of the metaphysical quandary and the deliberate thesis: is this a nightmare (Bérenger cannot arrive) or a problem (he must arrive)? The climactic scene with the killer provides the answer, for here again the play must choose: is Bérenger to die because of an irrational symbol or in order to state a social problem? Because it is Bérenger himself who states the social argument without awakening any comprehension in the killer, it is clear that this is a colloquy with the absurd. The killer stills Bérenger's efforts, and things are righted dramatically. The absurd remains one and unalterable.

But another Bérenger, that of *Rhinoceros*, is granted an assertion over the absurd. Whereas the very lighting and fiber of *The Unhired Killer* were the color of doom, they compose a pastel in *Rhinoceros*. When the first beasts start raising dust, the scene is not visibly affected—significance is slow in evolving out of the nonsense. There are three acts, and Ionesco is not at home in a long play.[14] Throughout the play, Bérenger is a singularly obdurate bourgeois, blinder even than his former incarnations. It is only at the very last moment that his eyes are opened: he is the last man. There remains for him only to assert his manhood. As the curtain comes down, his last words are, "I will not capitulate!"

Since the curtain is down, the last word remains with Bérenger. A statement greater than the predicament of man is allowed, and the predicament is voided. The viscous

[14] He himself admits this; see, for example, his interview in *L'Express*, Jan. 28, 1960.

dream is dissipated, and in its place appear the tangible objects of the bourgeois salon. In asserting himself, Bérenger asserts the limited reality of all things on his stage. The final image of the hero shows him firmly gripping a hunting rifle; it is well known that with the right gauge and a steady aim, it is possible to bring down a rhinoceros—the predicament has become a mere problem play.[15] After the première in Düsseldorf in 1959, it was quite apparent to a number of critics that the rhinoceroses were Nazis.

The primordial states of being and the absurd should not conceal the simple temptation of the thesis that is evident in Ionesco. With the second ringing of the front doorbell in *The Lesson*, a circularity starts that is the evidence of fatality—like the circular motion of the infernal machine in its unwinding (Cocteau's device for demonstrating the tragic mechanism) or that of Anouilh's tragic mainspring (*Antigone*). But when in *The Bald Soprano* the Martins replace the Smiths on stage as the curtain falls and their twaddle starts all over again, the circularity does not encompass fate; it circumscribes a much narrower area—that of social satire.

The conventional attributes of mediocrity stated for the sole purpose of destruction may become the sacrificial requisites of a metaphysical truth, but they are first, inevitably, the stuff of satire whose object is likewise the destruction of mediocrity. Before the monster implicit in the bourgeois interiors of Ionesco becomes explicit, there is only a bourgeois interior, and as merely a repository of human stupidity recognized, it disintegrates in satire; there will be no salon in later scenes—just a monster. It is therefore not clear why Ionesco remains so consistently a satirist, effecting his

---

[15] In *The Unhired Killer*, Bérenger had a gun also, but he realized that it would be of no use against the killer that was in his sights.

partial destructions within the comprehensive destruction of his full statement, although both are mutually contradictory.

Even the apocalyptic vision of Bérenger in *The Unhired Killer* is obscured by prior digressions. One of the characters says earlier in the play:

The real revolution is taking place in the scientists' laboratories and the artists' studios. Einstein, Oppenheimer, Breton, Kandinsky, Picasso, Pavlov, they're the ones who are really responsible. They're extending our field of knowledge, renewing our vision of the world, transforming us.

Either this melioristic optimism contradicts the end of the play, or the absolute negation at the end voids this optimism. The speech belongs to an episodic Man who is "very drunk." Are we then to reject the statement, even though Breton and Picasso are acknowledged forebears of the author? [16] There is no way of reconciling these conflicting views into a system. Ionesco's plays are interlarded with concerns that exclude the play. The most lethal development waits while the characters indulge in topical commentary or philosophical speculations—as absurd as this acknowledgment of an outer reality may be within the context of a negation that proposes itself as sole reality.

Since such statements are in no way connected with the play, they must be viewed as intrusions by the author, which, though they make no contribution to the organic meaninglessness of the play, are nevertheless not meaningful as credos.[17] Praising the praiseworthy (as above), lashing

[16] In "Expérience du théâtre," Ionesco says that Picasso has liberated painting by making it what it should be. And in *Victims of Duty*, the surrealists are given credit for a new and valid sort of theater.

[17] The statements are reminiscent of Ionesco's essays and interviews when he leans to the left in liberal papers ("The important

the usual whipping boys (in the same play, a former incarnation of Bérenger's concierge becomes a rabble-rouser in parody of Marxists in particular and revolutionaries in general), breaking the conventional lances in favor of minorities and the disinherited, Ionesco's beliefs boil down to a pap not unlike the views of Bérenger himself—or those of any other "little man" on these bourgeois boards.

The attentive eye which Ionesco keeps on the mundane affairs of the world from behind the shambles of his metaphysical stages takes in not only the political world but also the world of other dramatists, colleagues, critics, and spectators. Of these, Brecht has a talent for rousing his ire most frequently.[18] A play such as *The Alma Impromptu* is almost entirely devoted to making fun of Brecht's methods and conceits. He finds most amusing the thought that a spectator might be asked to return several times to the theater in order to assimilate a play; although he seems not to understand the role of the Brechtian actor, he thinks that it is ridiculous to speak of objectifying a role; he has people running about on stage with posters, in fine Brechtian fashion; he even makes fun of the *gestus* and the temptation of goodness.

thing is to find what there is in common between me and a shoemaker in the eighteenth century—and I believe that he resembles me," in *L'Express*, Jan. 28, 1960) or when he leans to the right in conservative papers or the left attacks him ("I am deeply suspicious of the so-called didactic theater—ideologists who are more Stalinist than was Stalin himself and dramatists who want to save the world at any price or educate it," in *Arts*, Jan. 20–26, 1960). See also his "anti-Stalinist" statements in rebuttal of Tynan's criticism in *The Observer* (see note 18).

[18] Ionesco has not, however, shown in his articles that he understands Brecht too well. He includes him in a list of so-called "new boulevard authors" in the rebuttal to Tynan (*The Observer*, June 1958); and in "Expérience du théâtre," he refers to the Brechtian actor as "a lifeless pawn, without fire, without participation or personal invention."

And yet, in Brecht, it is this temptation of goodness which signifies the intrusion of an irrational being against the desires of an author who had hoped to make a statement that would not be swayed by the human stage. The dimension of Brecht's plays is that of the tension between the control which he sought and the assertion of the stage which (because freedom is also a human principle) the author can never dominate fully.

Brecht spent his life in the theater, and his plays grew out of the dialectic of criticism and counterstatement. They are antipodal to the plays of Ionesco with their cavalier stage directions, their flippant commentary, and their careless construction.[19] In *Victims of Duty*, Madeleine says to Nicolas, who doesn't write because "we have Ionesco and Ionesco, that's enough": "[Since] the modern world's in a state of decay, you can always report on the process!"[20] (In the less flippant French: "You can be a witness to that decomposition.") One wonders at the word "modern." If decomposition there is, is it in the world—the modern world or any other? Or is it in man? In the same play, Ionesco scoffs at a medieval drama, *The Miracle of the Woman Whom Our Lady Prevented from Being Burned*, which to him is mere "naturalism," that is to say, "an investigation brought to a successful conclusion"—"If you forget that bit of divine intervention, which has really nothing to

---

[19] Ionesco cares so little for such details that he is likely to forget what he has specified, in the same manner as his characters who forget what they have just stated. In *The Lesson*, the murder weapon which is "indifferently invisible or real" becomes specifically invisible as the play progresses; in *The Future Is in Eggs*, the grandfather is consigned for good to his picture frame, but forgets this a little later and joins in the action; etc.

[20] *Victims of Duty* appears in *Three Plays* by Eugène Ionesco, translated by Donald Watson, published by Grove Press, Inc., Copyright © by John Calder (Publishers) Ltd. 1958.

do with [the play]." Yet in that play, as in classical tragedy (which Ionesco also dismisses, terming it "distinguished naturalism") and again as in Brecht, when the technician comes up against the irrecusable presence of a living person, is it not precisely a matter of divine intervention—or at least divine intervention to the extent that it can be effected on stage, through the intervention of man? Treating the play which he writes with casual indifference may state a part of the modern world's decomposition, but it cannot construct the play that will bear witness to that decomposition. That witness is human, and exists only in a human drama.

In the theater, tragedy is absurd. Man is wed to his anxiety, and the adversary with whom he contends is monstrous. But the tragic hero and his drama are economical. The dignity of the protagonist is at stake: he *must* remain alone. A lesser presence would lessen him, and he alone has sufficient stature to define his single opponent. It is known that he will lose this battle, and the play is final confirmation of this evidence. But he alone states the magnitude of his destruction, and if the disparity between him and his fate is comical, only he can fathom the depth of that laughter. Short of this, the drama remains self-conscious, "halfway between sincerity and parody," as is Bérenger's declamation (in *The Unhired Killer*)—a sterile middle ground on which the dramatic plant starves. The stage has been kinder to Ionesco than he has been to it, and it has often returned a human being for the antihuman which he sought. Without that human illusion there remain only a brittle laughter at shells and surfaces and a tinny word play—paradoxically, the childish fun which only intellectuals find amusing.

III ~ SAMUEL BECKETT:
The Difficulty of Dying

I remember his telling us the story of a little girl, very strange and unhappy in her ways, and how he treated her unsuccessfully over a period of years and was finally obliged to give up the case. He could find nothing wrong with her, he said. The only thing wrong with her as far as he could see was that she was dying. And she did in fact die, shortly after he had washed his hands of her.

Samuel Beckett, All That Fall [1]

THE "absurd" supposes a human judgment: only man can confront the disparity or experience the nausea which he terms "absurd." Short of this binomial—man and his awareness—there remains little more than a description of phenomena. No object is absurd until a man thinks it so; until then, it merely *is*—the absurd has no grip on it. To reason that the absurd stage must be a representation of the absurd is to neglect the syllepsis, man, that defines the absurd on stage and off. Life may be seen as futile play acting; but the stage that is supposed to be a representation of that life must be something more. Off stage, reality is stated in the human fact—a person; his "absurd" demise is in his inability to signify more than the illusory actor. On stage, that hollowness is not sufficient, for although it is a necessary part of the stage, it does not of itself provide the human

[1] *All That Fall* appears in *Krapp's Last Tape and Other Dramatic Pieces* by Samuel Beckett, published by Grove Press, Inc., Copyright © 1957 by Samuel Beckett, Copyright © 1958, 1959, 1960 by Grove Press, Inc. Other quotations from this translation are on succeeding pages.

opposition that names the absurd. The absurd is the province of man; make-believe, that of the stage. The stage can
be a metaphor for the circumstances of a man, but cannot
represent those circumstances until it represents a man. It
is thus legitimate to say that every dramatic representation
of man is, when successfully effected, a successful representation of the absurd. When it attains less, drama is less
than absurd. It may be comical, odd or merely chaotic—
absurd socially, not ontologically. When Ionesco denies the
possibility of a dialogue between his protagonist and the
antihuman on his stage, the antihuman figure materializes
the necessary Moira of tragedy. But if that antihuman
threat is essentially physical (in the form usually selected
by Ionesco it is the overwhelming expression of a physical
evidence), the overstatement of that evidence will cancel the
symbolic as well as the physical assertion of the human
being. If it does, the menace loses its human confirmation
and reverts to the dimensions of a mechanical phenomenon.

The brutality of French drama in the postwar years
derives in part from the physical explicitness with which
the symbol of the antihuman has been portrayed. Samuel
Beckett is one of those who have been fascinated by the
precarious world of the *Grenzsituation*, that moment of
dramatic equilibrium when the maximal statement of the
antihuman is still balanced by the evidence of its human
informant. After the first performance of *Waiting for
Godot*,[2] in 1953, and again after that of *Endgame*, in 1957,
critics were convinced that Beckett had contrived an absolute negation of human existence, a drama situated be-

---

[2] *Waiting for Godot* by Samuel Beckett, translated from the
French by the author, published by Grove Press, Inc., Copyright
1954 by Grove Press. Quotations in subsequent pages are from this
translation.

yond extinction. It took more time and other plays to draw their attention from the surface of these stagnant waters to the life of their microorganisms.

It was merely a matter of insight. That life was discernible from the first, even upon the barren flatlands of *Godot*, variously described as a platter (in the original) and a board. For upon this apocalyptic tableland of emptiness and desolation ("a road in the country, with tree"), there is a person, a Chaplinesque tramp—the parody of man as a clotheshorse, with bowler hat and outlandish shoes: upon this mockery of landscape is the mockery of a man. But in man, there is an inherent distinction, a significance which mockery does not dispel as effortlessly as it dispels the significance of the landscape. The tramp is Estragon, the tarragon of French recipes. He is joined by another tramp, this one with a Slavic name, Vladimir. These two will be witnesses to the ineffectuality of common sense (Estragon) and romantic notions (Vladimir).

A pair of battered shoes, the tramp's symbol, is the first center of focus—Estragon is trying to remove his. In the manner of every endeavor on this stage, even the most modest, it is a painful venture, and an unsure one. Estragon's first comment is, "Nothing doing." The words are echoed and amplified by Vladimir, one of whose romantic impulses is to discover a metaphysical significance to human utterances: "I'm beginning to come round to that opinion. All my life I've tried to put it from me, saying, Vladimir, be reasonable, you haven't tried everything yet. And I resumed the struggle."

These two are old acquaintances, but as they are no longer sure of their own identity, their relationship is in doubt. They spend the night apart and are certain only of intervening beatings, since they are breathing and life is an endless rain of blows. Suicide is a recurrent temptation, but it requires an assertion of which they are not capable. "We should have thought of it a million years ago, in the nineties. [. . .] Hand in hand, from the top of the Eiffel Tower, among the first. We were respectable in those days. Now it's too late. They wouldn't even let us up." At present, they merely wait for the ultimate extinction, a repose to which they look forward with longing and horror—and, withal, disbelief for having been frustrated too long.

Because he is of a speculative turn of mind, Vladimir considers briefly the possibility of Christian salvation, mainly as a way to kill time—the paramount activity during this metaphysical wake. But the very jargon of such speculation (salvation, hell, damnation, and so on) pales into meaninglessness because of the evidence of their being. Estragon, the realist, tires and declares, "I'm leaving"— and, since this is action, and thus an impossibility, "I'm not listening." The talk eventually bogs down in doubt over the account given by John of the Crucifixion, which, though generally invoked, is not confirmed by the Synoptics. "People are saps," concludes Estragon (the vulgarity of the French term is even more definitive), and again, he proposes to leave. At this point, Vladimir introduces a metaphor for their inaction: "We can't [leave]. We're waiting for Godot."

The wait continues. Estragon, the doubter, tires of talk, falls asleep, and is awakened by Vladimir, who still finds meaning in human contact. But he refuses to listen to Estragon's nightmare—the nightmare of their existence again renders futile the words they use and their evocation. Their thought reverts to suicide, and for a while, they evaluate their chance of escape by helping each other to hang from the tree. The futility of the plan is soon apparent. Their speculation returns to Godot who did not make an actual promise and who, before coming, must first consult his friends, his agents, his correspondents, his books, and his bank account: he is someone in the driver's seat before whom they are mere supplicants who have thrown away their rights.

Two other figures enter, two other nations, two more ironic iterations "of the same species" (and "made in God's image!"—this exclamation accompanied by "an enormous laugh"): Pozzo, the dark well of human misery, and the hapless Lucky, the former leading the latter on a rope to the market (at Saint-Sauveur, in the original—the Holy Savior's) in order to sell him. Lucky, the menial, carries the luggage; Pozzo, the master, a whip. Pozzo is talkative and brutal; Lucky is dumb but vicious. Reacting according to stereotype, Vladimir is appalled at the treatment to which Pozzo subjects Lucky, but when Estragon tries to wipe Lucky's tears, he is repaid with a stiff kick in the shins. Pozzo accepts things as they are. His illusions are only social. He describes his managerial miseries with sufficient conviction to turn the emotive Vladimir his way (thereby making an incidental comment on the value of Vladimir's emotions); he is a believer in the virtue of the managerial rites, the social histrionics, the niceties of formal exchanges, the reality of time. As an added graciousness, he offers his guests a dance by Lucky, the dance of the net, the self-entanglement of man within his circumstances.[3]

Lucky also thinks. In a now-famous monologue, he presents the oral counterpart of the dance within the net. The inconclusive thoughts of mankind about its lot are voiced

[3] The useless dance of humans is a recurrent metaphor of Beckett, who has written at least two mimes (*Act without Words I* and *II*) that depict the meaningless postures of living.

as by a defective record that reduces even the abortive
speculation to severed sentences and repetitive exclamations
—fleeting glimpses of a little "personal god" with a white
beard, an apathetic divinity, hell on earth as it is in heaven.
As the words tumble forth in an increased frenzy, the
convulsed thought becomes a chaotic landscape of lifeless-
ness and stones within which Lucky's stream is eventually
spent, running dry on the word "unfinished."

Lucky and Pozzo depart. A messenger announces the
postponement of Godot's visit: he couldn't come today,
he will surely come tomorrow. The sun goes down, and
the moon comes up, but the long-awaited night brings no
change. The tramps remain as they are, where they are;
the curtain comes down on a statement of their immobility.

The second act is an intentional redundancy. The place is
the same, and so is the hour—Pozzo's faith in his waistcoat
watch was no more than a social euphemism. Heels together, toes apart, the Chaplinesque shoes are near the
footlights. "The tree has four or five leaves" (the English
version corrects the original "covered with leaves"); a
meaninglessly new season confirms the cessation of time.
Echoing the circular motif, Vladimir comes on stage singing a ditty that is its own refrain. The two tramps meet and
enact once again the myth of human contact, playing out in
words the forms of social intercourse. For the unromantic
Estragon, all past events have been obliterated, and the
effort to make talk becomes painful once again. Their
isolation is tinted with the terror of *others*—the human
constant at the source of fear. Estragon breaks and sends
up a mournful wail to God.

Once again, Lucky and Pozzo cross their path. Pozzo
has become blind and, as befits symbolic blindness, his
inner vision has become more keen. When the tramps try

to draw him into the minuet of their small talk his clear sense of such futility breaks forth in anger:

Have you not done tormenting me with your accursed time! It's abominable! When! When! One day, is that not enough for you, one day he went dumb, one day I went blind, one day we'll go deaf, one day we were born, one day we shall die, the same day, the same second, is that not enough for you? (*Calmer.*) They give birth astride a tomb, the light gleams an instant, then it's night once more.

Pozzo and Lucky disappear; the ritual around the little "personal god" is about to begin. Vladimir faces up to it stoically; his sigh expresses the resignation that echoes down the modern wastes since Valéry: "Off we go again." The ritual ends—Godot will come tomorrow. The curtain comes down for the last time on the motionless figures of the two tramps.

To inquire whether *Godot* is a drama situated beyond extinction is to ask whether the sentence which the author imposes on his characters is such as to silence their meaning. The balance of optimism in tragedy is the extent to which a human affirmation exceeds the assertion of a human jeopardy: it is only when blinded that Oedipus asserts the full vision of a man. The pessimism of Ionesco demands the destruction of more than the physical human, since it defines the antihuman as that which can silence even the resonance of the human being against which it is matched. One may assert a world in which man can no longer make even the most limited assertion, but that view cannot find expression in the theater because its viability requires acceptance by the spectator of an essentially anthropocentric construct. Moreover, the antihuman incarnation of Ionesco derives its strength through specialization—it is the personal fate of only a single victim. Ionesco's drama supposes a victim suited to the manifestation of an absolute force that operates within narrow limits. There is no assurance that the spectator may provide such an ideal victim.

Aristotelian tragedy allowed between spectator and protagonist only the residual human bonds of pity and terror. In a drama whose terror pales with an awareness of the monster's limitation, the sardonic cheerfulness of the author dissipates what is left of the human illusion. The elimination of pity mutes within the spectator the last echo of a human evidence. Although terror and pity suppose two different reactions by the spectator (the god's eye being, in the first instance, that of an impersonal divinity; in the second, that of the kindred spectator), both are reactions to a strictly human dilemma. Until his epiphany makes him godlike, the protagonist of classical tragedy does not accept the dictates of the gods (excluding, of course, the protagonist of a religious play, such as Antigone). During the time of his ignorance, he acts as if he were able to assert himself; in his ultimate lucidity, he does. Even in the moment of tragic irony, *he* is not the one who falters; it is *the spectator*, who rises above the action. Such a protagonist is seldom divorced from his own humanity or the spectator's.

Until the second incarnation of Bérenger there is no epiphany for the people of Ionesco; they are innocents to the last. For those waiting for Godot, there is no revelation either—they are bitterly wise from the start. Each of these people is cut adrift. But the Irish playwright does not consider the fate of his characters with the same equanimity as Ionesco; this supposes an even more intensely pessimistic view of the human dimension—and a converse ability to view the human dimension of the stage with considerably more optimism, even though the world of Beckett does not undergo the degeneration from innocence to doom that marks the progress of Ionesco's action. Beckett's world is doomed at birth. It is a parodic symbol that denotes the same impotence as that of its people. It is flat (a board, a platter, and so on), sterile, and lonely: the single tree and its token seasons suggest its climate and topography. Its color is gray, that minimal tolerance of light sufficient to indicate the absence of color; the sky is alternately overcast or lit by a moon that is "pale with weariness." The hopelessness of every endeavor, the failure of every impulse turns the spiritual horizon dim and toneless, and the mimetic objects are similarly affected—the shoes of Estragon are degraded from an imagined brilliance (black or yellow) to the hazy middle region of gray. What color there is portends the cadaver, the greenishness of decay.

Decay results from too long a stillness; it is the evidence of cumulative frustration. In this drama of stagnation, what once was life is now putrefaction. The social fiber of these people has worn out: they are tramps. Their clothes are in shreds, their shoes are decomposing. So are they—they smell. Pozzo asks, "Which one of you smells so badly?" The answer is given by the realist, Estragon: "He has stinking breath and I have stinking feet." That putrefaction is the only physical evidence of their existence. In order to bring back the memory of their first encounter with Pozzo and Lucky, Vladimir reminds Estragon that he was kicked in the shins by Lucky. But Estragon has no memories and does not remember that either. Vladimir reverts to physical proof: "Pull up your trousers. [. . .] There's the wound! Beginning to fester!" The festering is Vladimir's triumphal evidence of continuity. As this is a play, the necesary extension of which is a spectator, that putrescence extends to the latter. In attempting to find his bearings, Vladimir surveys the meaningless landmarks that inevitably include the audience and, as is his custom, he turns to metaphor (even by inadvertence): "You recognize the place? [. . .] that tree . . . (*turning towards auditorium*) that bog . . ."

The world of Ionesco assaults, this one exhausts; both kill, the first by assertion, the second through silence. The world of Ionesco is constantly more full of objects, that of Beckett is a self-perpetuating desert. In the way of an isolation cell, it is bare of anything at which the prisoner might clutch. The toy monsters of Ionesco rely on the good will of the spectator. The wastelands of Beckett extend into the conscience of the spectators; he is a more universally terrifying author than is Ionesco.

The world of Ionesco is a becoming. The threat is pre-posited in *Godot*. It is a prison now, and it has been a prison for as long as memory can extend. Estragon has no past—it is all he can do to endure the present. Vladimir tries to awaken in him the memory of school days: was school godless? Estragon does not know whether or not it was godless. Vladimir concludes: "You must be confusing it with prison" (French version only).

If this metaphysical attrition is absolute, if there is no place to turn, nothing to grasp, death is the only answer. Repeatedly, Estragon assumes "a uterine position." But since death would be a way out, and there is in fact no way out, death fails him. Suicide is often attempted, always un-successfully; night never actually comes; Godot is never more real than a broken promise. Beckett balances his people on the outermost ledge of being, but never gives them the comfort of oblivion: he has achieved the litotes of tragedy, the horror of being—beside which death pales.

Merely surmising birth, but assuming a continual dying (though never death), Beckett peoples an agony of being,

an unrelieved topography of gray which now signifies the
minimal tolerance of life compatible with suffering. The
nightmare overspreads this comatose world drained of color
and void of levels and reduces to semantics the distinctions
between day and night, between walking and the fitful
moments of sleep. It is the evidence of a world in which,
by fiat, nothing happens and in which attempted action is
at most a brief heresy, something doomed that makes the
silence appear for a moment as an ironic commentary. It is
the substance of a play that neither starts nor ends, whose
talk (its only evidence) is a circle constantly coming to a
close, be it in abortive speculation such as that recited by
Lucky, in jokes whose punch line is forever missing, in
storytelling rondelets that end with the incident of their
beginning.

All growth is stunted. Vertical development is replaced
by a circular motive connoting the failure of assertion and
a void:

VLADIMIR: And where were we last night according to you?
ESTRAGON: I don't know. In another compartment. There's
no lack of void.

One of the reasons why Godot can couch his evasiveness
in precise terms is the failure of every precision:

VLADIMIR: He said Saturday.
ESTRAGON (*very insidious*): But which Saturday? And is it
Saturday? Is it not rather Sunday? (*Pause.*) Or
Monday? (*Pause.*) Or Friday?

It is both madness and cowardice to allow the slightest myth
to develop on this barren ground. Every statement, because
it is a statement, is a lie in this world that voids the statement and mocks the most rudimentary attempts at exist-

ence. The dull-wittedness of Estragon is his fundamental consonance; contrary to Vladimir, he refuses to allow the parody of an intellectual illusion to develop on this desert. It is he ("aphoristic for once") who speaks that lesson as a commentary on one of Vladimir's more sustained philosophical speculations: "We are all born mad. Some remain so."

The human intent has been frustrated so long that existence itself is doubted as an intellectual apprehension. Vladimir is warily pessimistic: "So there you are again." But Estragon has proceeded beyond even a mood: "You really think so?" His question is rhetorical but not humorous.

Since nothing on this stage supposes engagement or development, there is no symphony, merely a succession of isolated notes—the single utterance of all things and the single significance limited to the moment of that utterance. Each character wears a bowler hat; it fits each poorly, but it fits them all. In the second act, Vladimir and Estragon come across Lucky's hat, and for a while, the three hats circulate from head to head, original ownership having been forgotten: thought is circular. (It is at best mere talking through one's hat; Lucky's had been left on stage because, after vainly trying to dam Lucky's metaphysical outpouring, Pozzo had previously trampled on it in a fit of rage, yelling, "There's an end to his thinking!") But the one hat that decks the several faces of mankind asserts yet another synonymy, the single significance of man: frustration, pain, eternity—the circularity of being. Such had been the diagnosis of Pozzo upon first encountering the others: "You are human beings none the less. (*He puts on his glasses.*) As far as one can see. (*He takes off his glasses.*) Of the same species as myself."

Beyond that evidence, there is nothing. Human solidarity

is as meaningless a statement as the statement of man himself. The four clowns on this stage have difficulty maintain-
ing themselves on their two feet; but when they grab each
other for support, the human prop fails them and all land
on the floor. The tramps' shoes, unwieldy and ill-fitting, are
symbolic of the essential instability of the human construct.
The verticality of the cathedral once symbolized man as
aspiration; in this drama of waiting for an absent god, man
in collapse falls in with the circular motive of frustration.
A single linear statement contradicts the futile circle: it is
the projection upon this dead world of the human prog-
nosis, as accurate as it is bleak. Life endures only as the
anticipation of suffering; Pozzo comments as he relights his
pipe, "The second one is never so sweet [. . .] as the
first."

Estragon puts a poser to Vladimir:

ESTRAGON (*looking at the tree*): What is it?
VLADIMIR: It's the tree.
ESTRAGON: Yes, but what kind?
VLADIMIR: I don't know. A willow.

The personality of a tree is in its leaves, of which this one
is symbolically divested. As a tree, it is a failure (significantly, Estragon's question introduces yet another vain
attempt at suicide, a gesture which the tree inspires recur-
rently); its significance cannot be redeemed through botan-
ical classification. Therefore Vladimir brings forth from
within himself a name that designates the tree as merely
a necessary part of the landscape. He calls it a willow—the
tree that weeps. This is a form of animism to which Vladimir, the symbol of misery, gives its shape; but as an attempt
to designate reality, his words are a failure. He admits that
he does not know to what species the tree belongs, and it is

very likely not a willow. But it is characteristic of him that
he should even attempt to endow a part of the nightmare
with the illusory substance of words. They are an important part of his existence. In a world where death and hope
are both removed, the persistency of the human impuse is
evident in a repeated temptation to escape, the postulates
of existence notwithstanding. Estragon tries to escape more
directly; short of death itself, he assumes the fetal position
and sleeps. Or, if that is not possible, he turns his back on
the event, the speculation, or the threat, repeating his leit-
motiv, "I'm leaving." Such is the form of his escape fan-
tasies; for Vladimir, they are the sentences which he weaves
and which Estragon cuts off so rudely.

Vladimir knows that beyond the irony of his clearsightedness his words are constructing the simulacrum of
a parlor game to fill the otherwise unendurable void; but
it is not easy for him to draw Estragon into the game:

VLADIMIR: I hope I'm not boring you.
ESTRAGON: I'm not listening.

. . . . .

VLADIMIR: [. . .] Come on, Gogo, return the ball, can't
            you, once in a while. [French version.]

Pozzo, by contrast, is well equipped to play this game in
which he is thoroughly schooled:

POZZO (*looks at the stool*): I'd very much like to sit down, but
            I don't quite know how to go about it.
ESTRAGON: Could I be of any help?
POZZO: If you asked me perhaps.
ESTRAGON: What?
POZZO: If you asked me to sit down.
ESTRAGON: Would that be a help?
POZZO: I fancy so.

ESTRAGON: Here we go. Be seated, Sir, I beg of you.

POZZO: No no, I wouldn't think of it! (*Pause. Aside.*) Ask me again.

ESTRAGON: Come come, take a seat I beseech you, you'll get pneumonia.

POZZO: You really think so?

ESTRAGON: Why it's absolutely certain.

POZZO: No doubt you are right. (*He sits down.*) Done it again! (*Pause.*) Thank you, dear fellow. (*He consults his watch.*) But I must really be getting along, if I am to observe my schedule. [. . .] But I see what it is, you are not from these parts, you don't know what our twilights can do. Shall I tell you? (*Silence. Estragon is fiddling with his boot again, Vladimir with his hat.*) I can't refuse you. (*Vaporizer.*) A little attention, if you please.

From the mannerisms to the vaporizer, Pozzo draws on the complex equipment of a performer, spinning, primarily out of words (the last available commodity), an elaborate social web with which to mask the abyss. The fact of the abyss is temporarily less important than the success of the illusion that provides him with his moment of pathetic triumph ("Done it again!").

The play is thus a construct of words devised upon an absence or a void—an essentially comical endeavor. The words of this elaboration are, at a first level, merely treacherous, reverting to nonsense or evincing inopportunely a scatological meaning, causing the dancers of the pavane to slip upon an ever-present ordure. Puns, frequently fecal, dot the dialogue; names betray the namesakes (in the French version, two metaphysicians whose contribution to mankind has been primarily rhetorical, are named Fartov and Belcher); an innocent rejoinder comments sardonically upon its context (Pozzo's reply to Vladimir who has asked him whether he had good vision before he went blind: "Oh, it was a good one indeed!"—an approximative version of the French, "Oui, elle était bien bonne"). At a second level, the whole semantic construct becomes an inversion of Bergson's comic principle as these people are seen desperately attempting to graft human flesh upon something that is unredeemingly mechanical.

VLADIMIR: When I think of it . . . all these years . . . but for me . . . Where would you be . . . (*Decisively*.) You'd be nothing more than a little heap of bones at the present minute, no doubt about it.

ESTRAGON (*nettled*): So what? [This version incorporates one stage direction which is only in the original.]

Estragon's social pique endures even beyond human existence: structural concerns continue, the collapse of the structure notwithstanding. The grim fun of Beckett derives from this vicious circle, from the obstinacy with which the human urge conjures mirages whereby to maintain itself. One of the reasons for committing suicide by hanging is that, according to the legend of the mandrake, it promotes ejaculation. "Let's hang ourselves immediately!" exclaims Estragon upon hearing this item of folklore. His exclamation rings out in this desert, upon which he is an old man past caring, and calls for death. But then, of course, that very outcry too is merely a passing fancy.

The linguistic elaboration is a metaphor that comments upon the absurd view of those who endow their social posturing with an ultimate significance. But the characters of Beckett are not fooled: they know that they are seeking only a brief diversion and are, even so, conscious of the crudeness of their deception. They remain aware of their condemnation: their span of attention is limited, and their concentration on the game breaks down frequently. At such moments, abruptly, their words have another ring. There is no longer a game being played, they are fully steeped in horror, and their words suggest a gamut of reactions from the sarcasm of lucidity to the outcry of anguish that rises from depths that are beyond any vision. In an excellent article, Walter A. Strauss quotes from Beckett's study on Proust to illustrate a parallel development:

Habit is a compromise effected between the individual and his environment. [It] is the generic term for the countless treaties concluded between the countless subjects that constitute the individuals and their correlative objects. The periods of transition that separate consecutive adaptations [. . .] represent the perilous zones in the life of the individual, dangerous, painful, mysterious and fertile, when for a moment the boredom of living is replaced by the suffering of being.[4]

But if the protective screen is rent, it is not for want of care. At nearly any given moment, there is someone mending a part of the illusion:

VLADIMIR: Time has stopped.
POZZO (*cuddling his watch to his ear*): Don't you believe it, Sir, don't you believe it. (*He puts his watch back in his pocket.*) Whatever you like, but not that.[5]

Should that screen be rent nevertheless, the sight of reality fills the beholder with panic. And as the game is of such an insubstantial nature, the descent from play living to reality can be abrupt:

VLADIMIR: How time flies when one has fun! (*Silence.*)
ESTRAGON: What do we do now?

[4] "Dante's Belacqua and Beckett's Tramps," *Comparative Literature*, Summer 1959.
[5] The watch is a central prop among Beckett's symbols of uselessness. See, for example, *Act without Words II.*

VLADIMIR: While waiting.
ESTRAGON: While waiting.
                    . . . . . [They try to "do the tree."]
ESTRAGON: Do you think God sees me?
VLADIMIR: You must close your eyes. (*Estragon closes his
          eyes, staggers worse.*)
ESTRAGON (*stopping, brandishing his fists, at the top of his
          voice*): God have pity on me!
VLADIMIR (*vexed*): And me?
ESTRAGON: On me! On me! Pity! On me!

General disbelief in the game denies sooner or later
even the most rudimentary of relationships; the usual
climate of these plays is one of cruelty. Estragon tries to
wipe Lucky's tears and gets kicked for his pains. When he
later espies Lucky in a state of apparent torpor and tries to
avenge himself by returning a few kicks, he stubs his toe.
No physical reality underlies the construct of words. Part
of that construct, Vladimir's, defines human relationships
and the humanity of man. But when the blind (and cruel)
Pozzo is yelling for help in his misery, Vladimir continues
his talk, because there is nothing else. At times, this latent
cruelty takes on a more active form, either as the result of
exasperation (the animal need to contaminate another human with the venom of suffering) or, again, because of a
need to maintain the illusion of existence, to create through
inflicted pain an appearance of action, the speciousness of
an assertion.

The grim present is a mockery of that which defines the
human, and the future is a mere continuum. In order to state
the suffering of his people, Beckett cannot reduce them to
functional organisms adapted to this metaphysical void; he
must suppose them ill-adapted. He therefore develops the
tenuous image of an antecedent life, of a past humanity,
somewhere in the hazy realm of memory—a mist-covered

image of something lacking in the present. The sands that designate this desert were once seashore (the "sables" of the original) or the life-giver itself—the sea. Developing an inverted Platonism, the present longing constructs the dim archetypes of antecedent phenomena, a fullness remembered, whereby to define the actual void. In order to be more than a statement of facts, the present ugliness must be also the awareness of beauty inalterably dead; the present brutality, the absence of a love formerly possible. And in this macabre farce where dying replaces death, the sweet sorrow of a once-attainable extinction turns to horror the present immortality. Beckett's cosmogony contemplates no future, time does not move forward; instead, his expanding universe of sorrow is ever receding from the nebula of the potential.

The essential metaphor of *Godot* derives from this demise of possibility. For Estragon and, especially, for Vladimir (the one who finds transitory comfort in imagining), the waiting is not anticipation of something to come but rather of the moment when the cord of memory will be severed at last and they will have attained the nirvana of objects. The people of *Godot*, whatever the nature of their pastime, look ahead to pain with the sharpness of their reason, rather than backward to the source of their desire; this is why Beckett has been able to contrive a mood of nostalgia that excludes sentimentality. It is in this sense that one must interpret the retort of Estragon to Vladimir who has commented in a moment when the fabric of their play has worn thin:

VLADIMIR: This is becoming really insignificant.
ESTRAGON: Not enough.

The words also state the texture of the play, its lesson, and its extension into the spectator.

In deferring his appearance, Godot preserves his image—
the illusion of a salvation formerly possible. The Christian
form of the consolation is repeatedly subverted. Reference
has already been made to the doubt cast upon the Gospels
by the singularity of John's account. Its failure is now
drawn into a great circle of futility that humanizes the
myth so as to make it participate of the essential frailty of
mankind:

VLADIMIR: Christ! What has Christ got to do with it? You're
not going to compare yourself to Christ!
ESTRAGON: All my life I've compared myself to him.
VLADIMIR: But where he lived it was warm, it was dry!
ESTRAGON: Yes. And they crucified quick.

The revelation that came to Christ is extinguished in the
present suffering, and the cycle of frustration comes full
circle.

Pain being the residual expression of man, the animal
impulses persist. Anouilh's Antigone had said, "[Even]
animals would huddle together"; Beckett's animals do,
occasionally. In the depth of their despair, an animal anguish drives them toward each other as if communication
were possible:

ESTRAGON: [. . .] Let's stop talking for a minute, do you
mind?
VLADIMIR (*feebly*): All right. (*Estragon sits down on the
mound. Vladimir paces agitatedly to and fro, halt-
ing from time to time to gaze into distance off.
Estragon falls asleep. Vladimir halts finally before
Estragon.*) Gogo! . . . Gogo! . . . GOGO! (*Estragon wakes with a start.*)
ESTRAGON (*restored to the horror of his situation*): I was
asleep.

But even the androgynous urge is doomed, and the sardonic play analyzes the detail of its failure:

ESTRAGON (*step forward*): You're angry? (*Silence. Step forward. Estragon lays his hand on Vladimir's shoulder.*) Come, Didi. (*Silence.*) Give me your hand. (*Vladimir half turns.*) Embrace me! (*Vladimir stiffens.*) Don't be stubborn! (*Vladimir softens. They embrace. Estragon recoils.*) You stink of garlic!

VLADIMIR: It's for the kidneys.

Defining its worlds of being and pretending, *Waiting for Godot* is part tragedy, part comedy. Its barrenness situates the tragedy—an absence of objects, of words, of illusions in the line of vision. The construct makes possible the comedy—the pathetic evidence of the protagonists, the elaborate architecture of their words, their Promethean effort to reduce the cosmic nightmare to the dimensions of an acquired habit. But such moments are few; the stage remains essentially bare, and there is little upon which to catch laughter. In this landscape of mud and cold (the present definition of Canaan past, a land that was "warm" and "dry"), upon which a former image is at most the faint regret of what can no longer be, the Eiffel Tower or the Macon country [6] that focuses a moment of regret is a strangely vivid landmark upon the murky horizon. Seldom is the grim eye distracted from its vision, and then only through a parenthetical commentary and an allusion to another world beyond that of the play, briefly remembered:

VLADIMIR: You should have been a poet.

[6] It is actually "le Vaucluse" in the French text, an echo of Beckett's own wartime memories.

ESTRAGON: I was. (*Gesture toward his rags.*) Isn't that obvious?

Once more the play engulfs all time and, unto itself, becomes the only world. And within the nightmare, out of the suffering and the minimal nostalgia compatible with an appreciation of the present horror, the music of these spheres is heard. The wry, vulgar, essential stichomythy rises as a soothing incantation upon the endless sands:

ESTRAGON: In the meantime let us try and converse calmly, since we are incapable of keeping silent.
VLADIMIR: You're right, we're inexhaustible.
ESTRAGON: It's so we won't think.
VLADIMIR: We have that excuse.
ESTRAGON: It's so we won't hear.
VLADIMIR: We have our reasons.
ESTRAGON: All the dead voices.
VLADIMIR: They make a noise like wings.
ESTRAGON: Like leaves.
VLADIMIR: Like sand.
ESTRAGON: Like leaves. (*Silence.*)
VLADIMIR: They all speak at once.
ESTRAGON: Each one to itself. (*Silence.*)
VLADIMIR: Rather they whisper.
ESTRAGON: They rustle.
VLADIMIR: They murmur.
ESTRAGON: They rustle. (*Silence.*)
VLADIMIR: What do they say?
ESTRAGON: They talk about their lives.
VLADIMIR: To have lived is not enough for them.
ESTRAGON: They have to talk about it.
VLADIMIR: To be dead is not enough for them.
ESTRAGON: It is not sufficient. (*Silence.*)
VLADIMIR: They make a noise like feathers.
ESTRAGON: Like leaves.

VLADIMIR: Like ashes.
ESTRAGON: Like leaves. (*Long silence.*)

From the wastes, a poem is born, and beyond extinction a ritual is played out, an exercise whose exacting performance is its single justification. The last gesture of man, the final utterance of Beckett is a Mallarméan swan song, an assertion of futility that is necessary both because it is an evidence and because no resonance is more intense within the poet. The spectator is invited to co-perform a gesture in a vacuum, to objectify that which most fully defines him—his suffering—in the manner described by Sartre, "rhythmically, without complacency, without self-pity, with an arid pureness."

In 1957, with *Endgame*[7] (a play in one act, written in English), Beckett answered the critics who had said in 1954 that he would never write another play because it was impossible for him to go beyond the statement of *Godot*. In that *Godot* was indeed a tour de force—equipoise on the brink of that beyond which there is no longer drama—it was fair to surmise that Beckett could move neither back by mitigating his vision nor forward, short of turning his stage people into indifferent objects. Beckett chose to take the step forward and wrote a play which in some parts confirmed the critics but in others surprised them.

The difference between the two plays is prefigured by their respective settings: the meaningless outdoors of *Godot* becomes in *Endgame* an even more restrictive "interior"— the womb-shaped room visualized for it by Roger Blin,

---

[7] *Endgame* by Samuel Beckett, translated from the French by the author, published by Grove Press, Inc., Copyright © 1958 by Grove Press, Inc. Quotations in subsequent pages are from this translation.

the play's first director. The metaphysical wastes of *Godot* were, in fact, a prison as real as the walls of *Endgame*. In either case, the statement is absolute; the second represents a desire on the part of the author to underscore its italics.

Once again, the burden of dialectic rests on two principals and two secondaries. First, and center stage in a wheel chair, is Hamm, the Hamlet figure of this tragedy, the ham actor of Beckett's plays who, in the manner of Giraudoux's primeval couple, talks on even after God's wrath has visited Sodom and Gomorrah. Hamm is blind and a cripple, and in the usual way of this contagion, those around him are either cripples or in the process of becoming cripples. (The loss of physical equilibrium in *Godot* extended from the reacher to the one reached; in the novel *Molloy*, 1951, Moran, the pursuer, starts looking like his quarry, the lame Molloy; and the pattern will recur. In this world of dying, the decaying and suffering body is an image of the soul.) The parents of Hamm, Nell and Nagg, are stumps in two trash cans on the left side of the stage. The only one of the four who can move on his own power, Clov, has an epileptic gait—his legs are going lame.

If *Godot* represents the pastoral stage of Beckett's dramatic imagery, *Endgame* might be termed his drawing-room play. The previous nature symbolism becomes the symbolism of artifacts; claustration is represented by man-made objects; escape frustrated is a picture turned against the wall, windows beyond reach; human atrophy is a wheel chair; the relentlessness of the nightmare is an empty box of sedatives.

In the words which Edith Kern made famous in speaking of *Godot*, *Endgame* is once again drama stripped for inaction. Its only motion is provided by an analysis of dying. The soliloquies of Hamm and Clov, or their attempts at dialogue, are evidence of the circular pattern noted in *Godot;* wise in their pessimism, these talkers subvert the very formulations which they attempt. As usual, the supernumeraries provide a diversion which is no more than a prolongation whereby the play continues for yet a while without actual happening. Nagg rises from his garbage can asking for his pap, the food of degeneracy. Nagg is but a shell of the paternal image, a nagging mouth to feed, before whom Hamm is the Biblical Ham—he who saw the nakedness of his father and whose son was cursed by Noah. Through their greater torpor, the people of *Endgame* are still lucid:

HAMM: Scoundrel! Why did you engender me?
NAGG: I didn't know.
HAMM: What? What didn't you know?
NAGG: That it'd be you.

The hatred between progenitor and progeny is one of the hostile feelings that bind these people. Only between Nagg and Nell, the stumps in the ash cans, man and wife, is friction less apparent because of a dependency on the human illusion. Between them evolves the dialogue of senility— Nagg and Nell, talking debris upon whom there is already the decay of the corpse (later in the play, Clov lifts their lids and surmises that they are dead altogether). These dregs still have the effrontery to claim memories and shadow-dance the vague figures of life remembered, the sexual urge, and tenderness, climaxed by the strange assertiveness of the sentimental and sweet-senile Nell whose last words are a whispered injunction to Clov, the only one ambulant: "Desert!"

The central figure, Hamm, maintains the illusion of existence in the same manner as the other blind man, Pozzo.

He is principally a mythmaker and acor. He is engaged in a Penelopean labor of words, dim re-creations of a fanciful past that require an audience (and justify his name), the respect of certain postures (he desires his wheel chair to be in the exact center—of what is ironically a womb), and formal trappings such as Pozzo demanded. But his soliloquy outlives its trappings. It ends as the voice of a man alone in the silent womb: the garbage cans no longer respond, nor does Clov. And so the lucid figure performs the "old endgame lost of old" and draws his bloodstained handkerchief over his face. This gesture of waiting extends indefinitely the words of Clov with which the play started: "Finished, it's finished, nearly finished, it must be nearly finished"—to which Beckett adds in the French version, "it may finish."

As in *Godot*, the set and mood are the present horror, physically noted: gray light, ash bins covered with an old sheet, Hamm with his bloodstained handkerchief, and so on. "The whole place stinks of corpses," says Hamm. The romantic beach, a recurrent figure of regret in Beckett, is the sand at the bottom of the ash cans. Nagg develops an extended metaphor about their metaphysical dilemma, the joke of the Englishman and the tailor, all through which a silent Nell is entranced by a youthful vision of Lake Como: "It was deep, deep. And you could see down to the bottom. So white, so clean." Nagg's story meanwhile builds to its mirthless climax against which Nell again juxtaposes the words of her vision, "You could see down to the bottom," which disintegrate in the vulgarity of a *double-entendre*.

The tangible props of this drama are an indication of the proximity of its people to their memories—*Endgame* grows unexpectedly familiar roots into the present. The tramps of *Godot* expressed their isolation through a symbol; Hamm comments ironically, "No phone calls?" Therefore, the bleakness of their vision is not the single spiritual dimension of their prison. The high walls, the curtained windows, their crippled bodies mix awkwardly with the blind alleys of their questioning; that which is noncontingent is lessened by being stated through that which *is*.

Still, human anguish is expressed. The paroxysm of pain that culminates in Estragon's long moan to God is echoed by Clov, though here the complaint is against parties unknown. Since his only notion of existence is suffering, Clov tries to account for it on its own terms:

I say to myself—sometimes, Clov, you must learn to suffer better than that if you want them to weary of punishing you —one day I say to myself—sometimes, Clov, you must be there better than that if you want them to let you go—one day.

This is the negative tropism, the movement away from the source of pain, away from the "being there." In *Endgame* there is no "existent" such as Lucky; its four characters are sentient, in compensation for their greater individual brutishness. *Endgame* is a play of more immediate snarling, with less dependency (even of an illusory sort) on the human crutch. Cruelty is one of the few evidences of such a dependency:

HAMM (*his hand on the* [*toy*] *dog's head*): Is he gazing at me?
CLOV: Yes.
HAMM (*proudly*): As if he were asking me to take him for a walk?
CLOV: If you like.
HAMM (*as before*): Or as if he were begging for a bone. (*He withdraws his hand.*) Leave him like that, standing there imploring me.

But more frequently, and with more temper than in *Godot*, cruelty is an urge to throw off an excess of misery onto another victim.

NAGG: I hope the day will come when you'll really need to have me listen to you, and need to hear my voice, any voice. (*Pause.*) Yes, I hope I'll live till then, to hear you calling me like when you were a tiny boy, and were frightened, in the dark, and I was your only hope.

What Nagg wants is to return to the days of his own indifference ("We let you cry. Then we moved you out of earshot so that we might sleep in peace") now that he is the victim of his son's indifference, time being circular, events remaining the same no matter what their outward appearance.

Although it cannot comfort Nagg, the moment of terror comes to Hamm, as it did in *Godot*, when reality appears through intermittencies in the game playing. "What is going on?" asks Hamm, and Clov answers, "Something is taking its course." And against the unendurable "being there," co-operative play-within-existence is once again attempted so that the illusion might be given the seeming substance of a witness. But the attempts are even more abortive than in *Godot*. Nagg and Nell play only briefly, and even in that short time, Nell drifts off into her own private vision of the past. The Nagg-Hamm and Hamm-Clov relationships are filial and thus fraught with too much bitterness to be constructive, even though co-operative illusions are occasionally attempted such as when they try prayer, only to experience individually its failure. The most systematic effort is that of Hamm ("Ah the old questions, the old answers, there's nothing like them!"), whose first words and whose summation are those of the chess player turned actor: [8] "Me [. . .] to play." In him, as in Beckett himself, the narrative vice is deepest, recording against sense the chronicle of human frustration. It is the vice already noted by Vladimir, "We're inexhaustible," in echo of the definer Malone: "And if I ever stop talking, it will be because there is nothing more to be said, even though all has not been said, even though nothing has been said" (*Malone Dies*, 1952). It is the only reason which can be found for a play like *Endgame*, leading William Barrett to say of its author, "Beckett is one of those who is really living beyond despair."

Because the eye prevails over the illusion, the comic element in *Endgame* is understated. Laughter fails a first time for want of co-operation:

HAMM: No phone calls? (*Pause.*) Don't we laugh?
CLOV (*after reflection*): I don't feel like it.
HAMM (*after reflection*): Nor I.

Laughter, the expression of triumph, is ruled out by axiom, as in *Godot*. Nell analyzes the process:

NELL (*without lowering her voice*): Nothing is funnier than unhappiness, I grant you that. But . . .
NAGG (*shocked*): Oh!
NELL: Yes, yes, it's the most comical thing in the world. And we laugh, we laugh, with a will, in the beginning. But it's always the same thing. Yes, it's like the funny story we have heard too often, we still find it funny, but we don't laugh anymore.

Such laughter as remains in *Endgame* is of two sorts. The first is the short rattle, which, like the yawn—a recurrent

[8] "Endgame" refers to a chess situation in which the kings face each other with limited support. Cf. the notion of the chess game as one of the abstract posturings in *Murphy*.

motif—signifies the laughter's objectivity. The other laughter, that of the audience, is the result of puns, either the involuntary subversion of the words themselves, the words that destroy the utterer, or the willed pun in which the utterer consciously subverts a part of his world by way of commentary. These range from the effortless inversions by Hamm (about Nagg: "If age but knew!") to the more elaborate derivations. When Nell whispers rebellion to Clov, telling him to desert, he puns on the word so as to underscore the hopelessness of the injunction:

HAMM: What was she drivelling about?
CLOV: She told me to go away, into the desert.

Such acuity keeps in sardonic bounds the edge of their terror, their recurrent fear that the road to oblivion may be lengthened, that the whole process may be retarded, complicated, called into question. It may begin with something as apparently innocuous as a flea:

CLOV: The bastard!
HAMM: Did you get him?
CLOV: Looks like it. (*He drops the* [*insecticide*] *tin and adjusts his trousers.*) Unless he's laying doggo.
HAMM: Laying! Lying you mean. Unless he's *lying* doggo.
CLOV: Ah? One says lying? One doesn't say laying?
HAMM: Use your head, can't you. If he was laying we'd be bitched.

The room that confines the participants of *Endgame* robs them of a part of their dimension. It has been noted already that where the memory of the tramps was once sufficient only to give substance to the horror of the present, in *Endgame* memory endures in the notion of precise terms, in the usage of specific objects. The metaphysical confinement of the outdoors in *Godot* seems too frequently in *Endgame* to be simply the confinement of a room. The ugliness of the first was natural, and hence necessary, extending beyond what is visible; in the second, the actors seem to be isolated from their past by little more than the barrier of sordidness that delimits the "refuge." In the same way, the puns and the linguistic ritual that curtains their awareness find sustenance in these objects, and the play is not lifted beyond them to the level of poetry or of a universal concern. It remains instead curiously inorganic, the drama of overly specific individuals signifying nothing individually because of the object lesson which they are supposed to implement.

There is still, of course, the fear and the waiting. But because it is too much the statement of a private aberration, the dilemma loses some of its urgency:

HAMM: I once knew a madman who thought the end of the world had come. He was a painter—and engraver. I had a great fondness for him. I used to go and see him, in the asylum. I'd take him by the hand and drag him to the window. Look! There! All that rising corn! And there! Look! The sails of the herring fleet! All that loveliness! (*Pause.*) He'd snatch away his hand and go back into his corner. Appalled. All he had seen was ashes.

The madman's world states less about universal Chaos than it does about a single individual. A double problem is thus created, in that Chaos appears less terrifying as merely a private realm; and the aberrant individual, like those of Ionesco, is more easily explained away—he too is no longer *necessary*.

Even if such aberration did not single out an individual at the expense of the play, it would still force limitations on the dramatic expression of the human dilemma. One wonders whether the silence of God (Hamm: "He doesn't exist, the bastard!") can fully account for the anxiety of man. The repeated invective of Beckett in these two plays is too much a private (and Catholic) anger: it narrows considerably the extent of the quandary. The flea that threatens to reactivate the life cycle may well be more than a private concern of Hamm's. Expectation of doom is an oversimplification of man's anxiety, and hence of man himself. Added to the horror of his being is a recurrent suspicion in Hamm that even the full intensity of his single pain may fail to account for him:

HAMM: We're not beginning to . . . to . . . mean something?
CLOV: Mean something! You and I, mean something! (*Brief laugh.*) Ah that's a good one!
HAMM: I wonder. (*Pause.*) Imagine if a rational being came back to earth, wouldn't he be liable to get ideas into his head if he observed us long enough.

For Hamm, such "meaning" holds terror because it represents another detour on the endless way out; for the playwright, it raises a question of dramatic formulation.

According to its French theorists, modern French tragedy is one of exclusiveness. Aristotle's hero contained his tragedy—his flaw against his soundness. The tragedy of these modern theorists does not allow such a view of drama and offers instead a single path leading to a single issue. Ionesco's inexorable objects are its logical furniture and Beckett's functional anteroom ("Beyond is the . . . other hell") is its logical structure. In his *Antigone*, Anouilh speaks of the dignity of tragedy, the great silence that comes with its acknowledgment. That silence is the absence of a dialogue, the acceptance by the protagonist of a fate which he recognizes as his own. Oedipus is big because he asks questions that are reserved for the gods. He is not tragic for having killed his father and slept with his mother—he is tragic *before* these forfeits exacted by the gods from a human whose presumption appears to question their significance. The presumption of Oedipus is not an acquired trait, and he is in fact innocent; he has simply been too busy being Oedipus to think much about the gods of whom he is otherwise respectful. And so his tragedy begins at the juncture of his road and theirs, at his birth—many years before he kills Laius. Classical tragedy is fated: the gods predict that Oedipus will be a troublemaker, and they know that Antigone will be a human sacrifice. But Oedipus and Antigone are able to remain human; the presumption of Oedipus is never such as to make him assume that the gods know that he is presumptuous. In contrast, the Antigone of Anouilh knows quite as much as the gods: she and they refer to the "role" which she must play. There is no way out, therefore the silence, a sign of good breeding and good eyesight.

It is thus possible for Anouilh to view modern tragedy as an exercise in human dignity. Action, the belief by the protagonist that he is able to act, and tragic irony, the moment when that belief is stated by the protagonist, are replaced by waiting. The modern hero merely spends time between the postulate and the reckoning. His is a static moment in a drama of immobility—the silence of Anouilh or the obscene gestures of Beckett. Lost, in this theater, is the fundamental human impulse which Camus names revolt —not the revolt of Anouilh's Antigone against the order of yea-sayers, but the revolt against the human sentence itself, even when fully apprehended. Modern tragedy posits as total the circumstances of the hero; it fails to posit as total the persona in his refusal to accept his condemnation, in his rejection of his circumstances. The fully stated quantity in *Godot* is to be found not among its scarcely distinguishable people, but in the perfection of the flatness on which they perform. The absolute prisons of Sartre (*No Exit*) or Beckett (*Endgame*) define a limitation; if, as Hamm suggests, these prisons are metaphors for a human finite, then the absolute image can express only a part, and perhaps not the most important one, of that which it designates.

On commission from the BBC, Beckett has written two radio plays in English, *All That Fall*, first broadcast in 1957, and *Embers*, in 1959. *All That Fall* is the odyssey of Mrs. Rooney on her way to the station to meet her blind husband Dan. His train is delayed, as it turns out, because a little child fell out and was killed under the wheels. This scenario is steeped in the same gloom as the stage plays. Although the sun comes out for once ("Divine day for the meeting"), it does not remain long for Mrs. Rooney ("This dust will not settle in our time"). Hers is the common journey to extinction:

MR. SLOCUM: May I offer you a lift, Mrs. Rooney? Are you going in my direction?
MRS. ROONEY: I am, Mr. Slocum, we all are.

She is another of Beckett's liminal creatures, a cripple, fat to the point of immobility, isolated, half blind. Her way is dotted with a population of other cripples (Mr. Slocum: "I'm coming, Mrs. Rooney, I'm coming, give me time, I'm as stiff as yourself"), and as usual the human support fails. The paralysis of Maddy Rooney affects those who attempt to help her on her way: Mr. Slocum, whose car breaks down; Mr. Tyler, whose tire goes flat; Hetty Fitt, who, less symbolically, is wedged between the wall with Maddy who is trying to lead her up the station steps.

The metaphysical rot is in the June ditch full of the dead leaves of summers past, in the strains of "Death and the Maiden" briefly heard at the start and the end, in the rain—for even here, the sun glimmers only briefly—and the wind through which will drift the final strains of "Death and the Maiden" coming from a room behind whose shut doors a very old woman is suffering her agony alone. The dream is past and the longing for extinction has replaced it:

> MRS. ROONEY: Would I were still in bed, Mr. Barrell. (*Pause.*) Would I were lying stretched out in my comfortable bed, Mr. Barrell, just wasting slowly painlessly away [. . .]. Oh no coughing, or spitting or bleeding or vomiting, just drifting gently down into the higher life, and remembering, remembering . . . (*the voice breaks*) . . . all that silly unhappiness . . . as though it had never happened . . .

Dead voices sound in a dying world whose only semblance of life is the occasional pulsation of heat lightning, the flashing discharge of frustration too long pent up. Blind Dan blurts out:

> Did you ever wish to kill a child? (*Pause.*) Nip some young doom in the bud. (*Pause.*) Many a time at night, in winter, on the black road home, I nearly attacked the boy. (*Pause.*) Poor Jerry! (*Pause.*) What restrained me then? (*Pause.*) Not fear of man.

And now Dan Rooney has been involved in the death of a child, and the dual soliliquy climaxes in a burst of agonizing laughter by the two cripples, blind Dan and myxomycetous Maddy, both bent and helpless, as Maddy quotes from Scripture, "The Lord upholdeth all that fall and raiseth up all those that be bowed down." But the wild laughter is caught up in the wind and the rain, and it is on this lament, the ultimate commentary, that the incident closes.

The lesson is the same, but its texture and flavor are different, perhaps because of the circumstance in which these radio dramas were written. The soliloquy of Maddy Rooney would have sufficed for that lesson, or the couple's homophony, which is similar to the choruses of Vladimir and Estragon, of Hamm and Clov. Instead, *All That Fall* has a full cast of characters that are not simply functional. Instead of being metaphysical tramps or charismatic cripples, these are Irish villagers—a carter, a bill broker, a porter, a stationmaster, and so on. Instead of being intent on their single significance (or, more properly, their particular insignificance), they are particularized in ways that have no immediate relevance to Beckett's lesson; they have human twitches, such as the stationmaster who chews on his mustache in moments of stress. At times, they are people with such personal traits as to become near-caricatures; Hetty Fitt is a testy, hymn-singing, Protestant bigot who is as thin as a rail and absent-minded. Whereas in *Godot* four identical bowlers subsumed "all humanity," particular traits and accents in *All That Fall* signify nothing more than the description of an Irish landscape. The dilemma of "all humanity" waits on the personal definition of a number of individuals: the misery of existence has a Celtic note to it.

Embers is an evocation of a different sort. The many dead voices that surround the hero and feed his endless soliloquy are part of the selfsame screen already hung up by other protagonists to hide an identical doom, the fabric of words whose every syllable is a second gained on eternity. The people that lend their presence to the inner silence of Henry and his desperate dependence on them bring to light an aspect of man hitherto missing in Beckett's delineations. Henry's bitterness never displaces his human need. What his vision loses in clarity contributes to a human dimension; Henry attains the extensions of a man as the seer fades.

That occasional symbol of nostalgia in *Godot* and the present death of a life remembered in *Endgame*, the sea, is at the very center of *Embers*. It is an ambiguous symbol, whose sound and motion are those of life. But, in the words of Ada, Henry's wife, "It's only on the surface, you know. Underneath all is quiet as the grave. Not a sound. All day, all night, not a sound." It is still the tomb which the participants of *Endgame* could see through one of their windows, but nevertheless, it is the life-giver, and the memories it evokes are more than that which defines, through absence, the quality of a present misery. At least once, the sea roars into the present doom, in the climatic moment of the embrace of Henry and Ada when love was an assertion that blinded them to the vanity which all assertions must ultimately be.

Closer to the evidence of his sea-born vision and closer to the human figuration of that vision, the language tissue of Henry's existence is different from that of Hamm or those waiting for Godot. Theirs had been an exercise, the impersonal callisthenics performed singly or collectively while waiting. But the doom of Henry is personal. It is the extinction of his own world, a cadaver that has meaning only for him; its roots are in his past and his nerve tips. Hamm, Clov, Vladimir, Estragon, and the others are lucid; were they to advance but a single step more into the objectivity of their vision, they would move beyond the world of beings into that of objects. Henry, whose illusions persist in spite of his clearsightedness, has retreated a full step back into humanity.

What has been returned from the pronouncement to the

pronouncer, the predominance of human instinct over judgment in the principals of *All That Fall* and *Embers*, contributes to the significance of *Krapp's Last Tape*,[9] a playlet first performed in London in 1958. Of this play, as of all those preceding, critics have said that it is the final glimmer of life on a stage already wholly dark. As a matter of fact, *Krapp's Last Tape* is open to an entirely different interpretation.

Externally, Krapp is another of the sordid indwellers who went from metaphysical abjectness to physical degradation as they came indoors. He is "grimy," "dirty," with "white face. Purple nose. Disordered grey hair. Unshaven." His sight is failing, as are his ears and legs—the usual image of a present senescence. But as was the case of Maddy Rooney and Henry, this degeneration is no longer a metaphor for the human condition as much as it is a private realm to be entered upon for a more immediate and less metaphysical appreciation of that condition. Krapp has a name, an occupation, and a past; he is a writer, playing out a drama of constipation at a table center stage under a single light bulb.

The constipation of Krapp is significant: it removes the charismatic image from him and is alluded to throughout the play—in his name, the bananas that are a vice which he painfully resists, the "unattainable laxation," "the iron stool," and so on. Krapp is a man who cannot eject his existence, and since he has reached the vegetative state between an antecedent nirvana and the hell to come, his only motion is circular and mental—symbolized and suggested

[9] *Krapp's Last Tape and Other Dramatic Pieces* by Samuel Beckett, published by Grove Press, Inc., Copyright © 1957 by Samuel Beckett, Copyright © 1958, 1959, 1960 by Grove Press, Inc. Subsequent quotations are from this translation.

by the tape recordings of a former time which he plays in order to fill his present void (the play is set during a "late evening in the future"). The ironic futility of this mechanism is at first punned on by Beckett: "With all this darkness round me I feel less alone. (*Pause.*) In a way. (*Pause.*) I love to get up and move about in it, then back here to . . . (*hesitates*) . . . me. (*Pause.*) Krapp." But whereas Hamm, Estragon, and Pozzo seldom progressed beyond the yawn, Beckett is proposing for Krapp an entirely different outlook.

The story of Krapp is simple; it is told by another Krapp, thirty years younger, speaking through the tape recorder:

What I suddenly saw then was this, that the belief I had been going on all my life, namely . . . (*Krapp switches off impatiently, winds tape forward, switches on again*) . . . great granite rocks, the foam flying up in the light of the lighthouse and the wind-gauge spinning like a propeller, clear to me at last that the dark I have always struggled to keep under is in reality my most . . . (*Krapp curses, switches off, winds tape forward, switches on again*) . . . unshatterable association until my dissolution of storm and night with the light of the understanding and the fire . . .

At thirty-nine, his youth spent by even the most generous estimate, Krapp has given up the instinctual being that kept in bounds the suspicion of its futility and has become instead, like Beckett himself, the chronicler of his inner darkness. This is the moment of his lucidity, "the light of the understanding and the fire." It is then that the monologue begins. But Krapp, with Maddy Rooney and Henry, is among those able to cultivate this intimacy into a semblance of bloom. The objective creations of Vladimir ("return the ball, can't you"), Pozzo ("a little attention, if you

please"), Hamm ("I've got on with my story"), and Dan
Rooney ("Where was I in my composition?") are all ends
in themselves. But Krapp's ruminations are self-contained,
issuing from the wellsprings of his being.

Moreover, Krapp is not intent upon his present being;
he is the first to commit himself to the nostalgic illusion as
against his symbolic representation. His epiphany of darkness, the moment of recoil from life (recorded in his ledger
as "Farewell to love"), the moment when he presumably
turns to writing, does not account for his final delineation.
Since then, it is true, he has spent thirty years at this table,
confined to the hopelessness of this circular motion. But
the play does not close on a long, sober view of the unending spiral. The present is merely a mockery of a reality
past; that past is a myth whose assertion dwarfs into insignificance present gestures. Krapp has sold seventeen
copies of his book, "eleven at trade price to free circulat-
ing libraries beyond the seas." Of the ex-author, he has a
residual pleasure in words, verging on senility: "Reveled
in the word spool. (*With relish.*) Spooool! Happiest moment of the past half million." Of the young man, there is
the grisly caricature of the act of love with a "bony old
ghost of a whore." These he rejects, and, turning his back
on them, he moves into the past, the moment which he dismissed thirty years ago for the morose blackness of this
extended present. And as he plays over and over the tape
of his last encounter with the girl whom he left for the
dark fire inside him, the motions of the living water are
once again around him and the poetry of a more gentle
season with its flowers, its color, and its warmth carries the
old man away to the ultimate moment of his youth, living
anew "all that old misery"—a misery that had savor, the
lack of which defines the present absence. It is into that

world that Krapp returns; the grim irony which the present once asserted in *Godot* is absent. The present bitterness and the final irony are for the spectator alone:

Here I end this reel. Box . . . (*pause*) . . . three, spool . . . (*pause*) . . . five. (*Pause.*) Perhaps my best years are gone. When there was a chance of happiness. But I wouldn't want them back. Not with the fire in me now. No, I wouldn't want them back. (*Krapp motionless staring before him. The tape runs on in silence. Curtain.*)

Critics have noted the pairs on these stages—Vladimir and Estragon, Lucky and Pozzo, Hamm and Clov, Nell and Nagg, Maddy and Dan Rooney, Krapp and his tapes— which they have recorded as a persistency of the futile dialogue. As each dialogue is not of the same quality, it would seem instead that they come about primarily as the result of dramatic necessity: each may be viewed as a monologue in dramatic form (which reverts to a single voice when there is no dramatic necessity, as in the novels). Beckett has been concerned only with the soliloquy which, in its various keys and resolutions, attempts, if not always to answer, at least to witness the full intensity of the quandary and the suffering here below. It would be too much to say, as does Sartre's Roquentin, that this ordering within Chaos might be therapeutic, but it does nevertheless represent a conscious and complex ordering. Beckett is a gifted playwright, weaving the spectator into the texture of his drama, using the full dimensions of the stage for his effects. It is a drama which is singularly suited to the stage since his people are the actors either of a conscious pantomime or of a prior moment of being. Not only are they actors, but their world is a stage with its captive audience, its deceptive props, its illusory limits wherein is trapped the human consciousness. In a moment when the deception fails, Vladimir and Estragon are panic-stricken and the stage suddenly turns into a snare. Estragon runs to the backdrop and gets tangled in it (in the original play only). Vladimir drags him away, toward the spectators: "There! Not a soul in sight! Off you go! Quick! (*He pushes Estragon towards auditorium. Estragon recoils in horror.*) You won't? (*He contemplates auditorium.*) Well, I can understand that."

As the play of conscious actors, this drama can achieve only one dimension. At this level, the stage is able to show only a parody of the person with whose full dimensions it is concerned. But as the stage comes to signify and to embody the world of the spectator and as the spectator is drawn into stage action with his own totality, the play starts acquiring a more essential depth: from symbol, the actor changes into a symbiotic organism fastening upon the reality of the spectator. Mrs. Rooney, whose suffering is perceptible because it has the intimate shape of an Irish community; Henry, whose loss and need are evidenced in human voices; Krapp, who rejects the symbol for a common memory— these are people whose misery is more than a general commentary. They are the embodiments of a pain that is contagious. There is evidence in *Krapp's Last Tape* that the mere business of waiting and the sardonic commentary that occupies the interim may yet be expanded by Beckett to account for the more generous dimensions of the human potential.

Whatever temptation a more complex person may provide for Beckett, it must be noted that *Happy Days* [10] (1961) resists that temptation and, dramatically, marks

[10] *Happy Days* by Samuel Beckett, published by Grove Press, Inc., Copyright © 1961 by Grove Press, Inc. Quotations in subsequent pages are from this translation.

time. The play toys for a while with the human assertion, but rejects it for a statement of the usual paralysis by the usual innocent: Winnie, a woman about fifty, is imbedded up to above her waist in a mound. The Eleatic argument of immobility is still expressed by Beckett's version of Achilles and the tortoise—death is forever on the way but never arrives. In Act II, Winnie is imbedded up to her neck, but the play continues.

The monologue is familiar. The social tropism persists in spite of irrefutable evidence that existence is a mockery. Like the other characters of Beckett's drama, Winnie is fluent. And she also commands, as once did Pozzo, the elaborate paraphernalia of the social ritual, a literal bagful of tricks. These are the social level of her self-deception, the gestures that are rendered grotesque through the failure of any meaningful reference. In the face of annihilation, toothbrushing is nearly obscene. Beckett underscores the futility of this preoccupation by having Winnie interrupt her metaphysical commentary in her concern to find out what it is about the toothbrush that is referred to as "genuine pure . . .". At the nonsocial level of her speculation, she shares in the literary deception already noted in other plays of Beckett, the belief that as a poetized fiction life can be rendered more endurable or meaningful. Winnie is kept ecstatic by instances of "the old style [. . .] the sweet old style" and its clichés, some of which are deliberately literary, the mental counterparts of the toothbrush.

Winnie has a husband, Willie—one of Beckett's congenital cripples whose debility needs no props for its evidence. Once again, names show these people to be the complements of a monologue. The "happy days" to which the title refers ironically are the moments when the illusion of communication is indulged. But Willie's occasional monosyllables serve only to emphasize Winnie's isolation. Yet *Happy Days* is a comedy. The consciousness of death is a truth sufficiently intimate to link in a single reality character and spectator; it is out of this awareness that tragedy develops. When blindness cancels the unpleasant awareness, not only does a lighter mood settle on the stage, but also the spectator is separate from the incomplete character. The stage is set for comedy. In *Happy Days*, the title and the mechanical pursuits of Winnie outweigh her moments of awareness and tip the scales on the side of comedy. Furthermore, the physical stage is less sordid; and for once in a Beckett play, the human being is seen prior to decomposition—the heroine is an attractive woman. Puns are still there, but less frequent; laughter is not meant to break against the gloom. The pervasive irony of the play suggests humor of another sort, less violent and more sustained—the death rattle is now merely the patter of a silly woman whose fun and meaning derive from the disparity between what she says and the world in which she says it. Still, those critics who have seen in the play a departure from the old Beckett are referred to the final tableau:

Pause. Happy expression off. She closes her eyes. Bell rings loudly. She opens her eyes. She smiles, gazing front. She turns her eyes, smiling, to Willie, still on his hands and knees looking up at her. Smile off. They look at each other. Long pause. Curtain.

The final note is one of awareness that reduces Winnie's previous actions and words to nought. She ends as one of the conscious spinners of sounds and gestures before a familiar doom.

Beckett had a choice. In the feminine reality of Winnie, in the endurance of her social tropisms, Beckett could have seen a human assertion and a persistency that is its own justification and significance. But Beckett reduces the femininity of Winnie to empty gestures, the kinematics of the object. Winnie's plumpness, her bare arms and shoulders, her "low bodice, big bosom," are buried in Act II; if she is "well preserved," it is a mere irony, the author's view of her present situation. Her human reality, the brief glimmer of her sexuality, is extinguished in the *thing* which she becomes, the gestures that have no meaning, the hopelessness of her words. The spectator is reminded that even though the play escapes from the confining womb, the ash cans, and the wheel chairs and is set in the open, the grass is "scorched," the landscape is artificial ("maximum of simplicity and symmetry"), and the unbroken plain and sky are "pompier trompe l'œil." This world is as dead as the objects which its people have become. Even the unusual light is deceptive—it burns Winnie's parasol to a crisp. We are indeed close to hell, a feeling intensified by the customary references to a malevolent divinity: "How can one better magnify the Almighty than by sniggering with him at his little jokes." The human evidence apparent in Krapp and the nostalgia that is his ultimate expression are noted here as merely self-delusion and, in the end, become the steady gaze into oblivion.

Nevertheless, one cannot overlook the embers in the dead ash which this play adds to Beckett's cinerarium. They gleam briefly in most of the author's plays since *Endgame* and sometimes, as in *Krapp's Last Tape*, with enough force to suggest a source of light. The final verdict may not yet be in for Samuel Beckett.

IV ~ JEAN GENET:
The Difficulty of Defining

Such a definition of violence—through so many contradictory examples—shows you that I shall use words not in order to better describe an event or its hero but in order to provide instruction about myself. To understand me, complicity on the part of the reader is needed.

JEAN GENET, *The Thief's Journal*[1] (1949)

THE stage may probe a man at several levels, the most superficial of which reveals his familiar gestures, appearances, and crises; if that man has any significance, it lies beyond these. For Beckett, the stage extends his most compelling obsession; his need to record a Pascalian horror of the infinite emptiness becomes novel or drama according to the form of his chronicle. A stage of this sort stipulates for the actor certain motions, whose reality is the author's emotion that shapes them and the reawakening of that emotion in the spectator who interprets them with his own anguish. Halfway between the author's anguish and the spectator's is an animate object, the actor, the burning glass that consumes without being heated. An intellectual and a humanist, Brecht could not accept such a role for the actor; the actor as object was betraying his social function, his human rights. Instead, Brecht wanted for that actor *on stage* the full dimension which he enjoys *off stage*—he wanted him to be a commentator upon his own action. There enters into such a social desire a certain amount of dramatic logic: the animal

---

[1] To be published by Grove Press, Inc., translated by Bernard Frechtman.

reality of the actor will assert itself to a degree in even the most mechanical of performances. But once the actor turns commentator, he breaks the transmission that links playwright and spectator (at the expense of the playwright, incidentally) and alters wholly the dramatic process. If the actor grows into something more than the passive instrument of a rehearsed performance, he intrudes into the theater an alien whose definition—his personal reality—is not derived from the dramatic act. Instead of being described by the theater, he is now the one who as an outsider describes the theater, and thus he changes it into something else for which a new name would have to be found; he is breaking the ritual and altering the theater's mysterious balance of reality and irreality by adding over-assertively to its reality.

There is yet another level at which the stage may probe a man, this time through indirection, as ritual. The exact repetition of a gesture occurs either because that gesture was first deemed significant enough to be isolated from the run of gestures or because the act of exact repetition endows it with significance. Whatever its genesis, the gesture repeated is sterile as praxis; its only meaning is in its sacred significance as reiteration. The dramatic act is a ritual, learned, rehearsed, and performed, in a world calculated to encourage its mystery—the spectator's isolation, darkness, nighttime (it is a ritual with which the Brechtian actor would interfere because of his independence). Mystery and sacredness suggest areas not normally traveled by man: the ritual thus proposes to reveal something to man which is not normally his. The absurd condition of man, in one of Camus' instances, derives from his inability to know that which he must define as ultimately unknowable, while being unable to accept the evidence of his limitations. Man is ignorant of all ultimate truths, but some escape from his grasp more immediately than others. The more immediately apparent an object of ultimate ignorance is, the closer it is to sanctity—the only enzyme that might assist in what is beyond man's power to digest. Camus' man knows only that his system is alive in response to a limited stimulus. His practical knowledge is the hypothesis that such stimuli may affect similar organisms in a similar way; his wisdom comes from knowing that these areas of stimulation are inadequate to the elucidation of any meaningful truth other than the actual evidence of the disparity between his thirst and his attainment. This revelation of a truth which he cannot grasp is his to feel at any privileged moment; for Camus that moment precedes his revolt. For others, it may be latent in privileged objects or ceremonial, the object which is sacred defining itself as such because it proposes that revelation.

If the drama is returned to the stage and becomes ritual, the actor may well be its sacred object. Such an actor must proceed in a way directly opposite to the one suggested by Brecht: he must be consciously the unconscious object. Jean Genet, like Jean Cocteau and like Antonin Artaud before him, demands a magic stage and a sacred dummy as actor. He has been explicit about his ethics and his esthetics (and were there to remain ambiguities, Sartre has analyzed them in a closely packed book of some magnitude, *Saint Genet, Comedian and Martyr*, 1952). Genet is an outcast amid outcasts, a criminal and a pederast—outlaw to society, female to the fraternity of outlaws. When he writes for the stage, he wants his writing not to be fiction, not to be entertainment, not to be a mirror held up to whatever the stage is supposed to mirror, but to be a genuine act of aggression; his play is the continuation of a gesture performed by an outlaw against society.

No social protest enters into this outrage; Genet needs the existing order of things. He is Lucifer turned Satan, an aristocrat of Evil—the inverted world in which he dwells—and cannot desire to right the social structure without jeopardizing that which confers upon him his titles of nobility. "When [you undertake to accomplish] Evil, you still do not know what It is about. But I know that It is the only thing that has sufficient power to communicate enthusiasm to my pen, a sign, in this case, of my fundamental allegiance" (from "The Criminal Child," a speech requested of him by the French broadcasting services, but never allowed on the air). For Genet, Evil is the resplendence of Lucifer, the criteria evidencing the beauty of an act, an object, or a human being. Society is a sealed package, familiar, drab, secure—scarcely the right climate for what should be alive, significant, beautiful. Beyond this closed and sterile world is another into which society cannot expand without disintegrating; that outer planet is its mystery, short of which there is no poetry—something which society is intent on destroying but which is also its secret fascination. The outlaw inhabits this exotic world, and this is his first virtue. His second virtue comes from being the only one possessed of "that will, that daring to pursue a destiny that is against all rules" ("The Criminal Child"). These words should not, however, imply volition: the criminal is the one *necessary* being, the one who has not been shaped with another end in view. His is a world of subversion and death and beauty. The "saintliness" of the criminal (the two terms are frequently linked by Genet) is his rigor in not returning to the blandness of society, in resisting its blandishments.

But it is not a systematic evil which Genet will pursue in his drama: this is not a moral theater, even in reverse. Genet has a string of prison sentences sufficiently long to evidence the sincerity of his criminal leaning. It is not the crime itself that he will propose as an artist, but the flavor of crime; not the subversion, but the beauty of an order subverted. The ritual of this stage, its properties and actors, will be the sacred objects that reveal the mystical horror, the dread, and the supreme beauty of that which is beyond the usual purlieus of man (sometimes simply because it is beyond those purlieus). To begin with, in the image suggested by Sartre, Genet will redeem for man those false objects which God cannot see (since they are false) and which only man can contemplate as beautiful. He is able in this way to assume a beauty that exists only for man, and he achieves in so doing the touch of the esthete that turns into something imaginary what would be otherwise real. Much that defines the world of Genet also defines poetry.

But such objects cannot have the stillborn dimension of static things. Their reality is in their symbiotic relation to man, meaningful only as long as a human being anticipates their promise and is frustrated by their refusal ever to keep that promise. Only man can provide such a victim for the never-familiar talisman that remains both human, because of its human respondent, and more than human, because of its own ultimate unresponsiveness. The sacred object on stage touches man only in that part of him that strains to transcend his human essence. Genet's is an esthetic drama in which the spectator remains conscious, in his identification, of his necessary detachment.

Analysis of a play by Genet is most difficult in its incipience: how does one enter Genet's maze of interreflect-

ing mirrors? His first play to be performed was *The Maids* [2]
(in 1946). Somewhere between the statement of the stage
and Genet's conjuring upon it, the following action takes
place: in a woman's bedroom (Louis XV furniture, lace,
flowers), Claire, a young girl, is dressing. She is attended
by a maid, Solange, who appears devoted, loving, troubled,
and, ultimately, domineering; she insists that Claire wear
a red evening dress instead of the white one which Claire
wants. Claire is addressed by Solange as Madame, and from
their talk, it becomes known that Monsieur—Madame's
husband or lover—has been arrested, after having been de-
nounced to the police by Claire. The attention lavished by
Solange on Claire is a complex of love, devotion, and resentment, culminating in a verbal and actual slap: "You
think you can deprive me forever of the beauty of the
sky?" The scene is interrupted by the jangle of an alarm
clock, causing "the two actresses, in a state of agitation [to]
run together. They huddle and listen": they are maids
masquerading as mistress and maid while their mistress is
out.

They are in fact sisters and, back in their own world,
busy themselves so as to remove the traces of their play,
but they remain worried that some telltale clue might remain undetected to give them away. They are dominated
by the invisible presence of Madame who is about to return
and whom they both fear and love, as they alternately fear
and love each other. Madame is handsome, rich, good, and
gentle, but her virtues devolve from another world and
are not sufficient to mitigate the resentment of the maids at
being excluded from that other world. The resentment of

[2] *The Maids* appears in *The Maids and Deathwatch* by Jean
Genet, translated from the French by Bernard Frechtman, published by Grove Press, Inc., Copyright © 1954 by Bernard Frechtman. Quotations in subsequent pages are from this translation.

the elder sister, Solange, is such—she says—that she has attempted to kill her mistress, and Claire feels that in their ceremonial impersonations it is she, Claire, at whom Solange is striking through her mistress. Solange admits this: "Yes, I did try. I wanted to free you." The phone rings. It is Monsieur, who has been released from police custody, and Claire's denunciation may backfire. But there rises now in Claire a cool homicidal will: they will put an overdose of Madame's sedative in her linden tea.

The front doorbell rings. It is Madame returning, a fur-clad figure of chatter and superficial feelings. She has been seeing people about getting Monsieur freed. She is a mixture of kindness, utter indifference, nervousness, and, ultimately again, kindness. Solange enters with the lethal tea, but by now, Madame has tired of her role as actual mistress. Symbolically, she gives the ceremonial red dress to Claire, her furs to Solange. It is then that she notices the telephone receiver that has been left off the hook. The maids blurt out the truth: Monsieur called to say that he is free again. The world is returned to its normal order. Madame takes back her furs in order to meet Monsieur at the designated rendezvous. She leaves without drinking the tea. The two maids are once again alone. They will now have all night in which to perform the ritual of their impersonations. But there is a renewed sense of urgency in them. They pass over the time-consuming preliminaries and move directly to the moment of invective when Claire as Madame looses her contempt on her maid Solange. Solange, working up to a culmination of hatred, takes a whip and lashes a recumbent Claire. As Solange reaches her frenzied climax, Claire is slowly sinking into a mysterious illness—she is sick, about to vomit . . . The rage of Solange breaks, and she compassionately leads her sister off stage, into the kitchen.

Solange reappears alone after a few moments and speaks the soliloquy of liberation, addressing an invisible audience. She says that Madame is finally dead, strangled, and Solange exults in the splendid isolation of the criminal: "And who could silence me? Who would be so bold as to say to me: 'My dear child!' " She enlarges the size of her private public, moves out onto the balcony, and with her back to the spectators addresses all the shadowy people that crowd her night. She enacts in speech her triumphal procession up to the gallows, moans briefly over poor Claire—even as Claire silently comes into the room and, leaning against the door, listens to her sister. Solange continues awhile longer and then, without surprise, turning to her sister, says: "Claire . . . we're raving." Claire, in a sad but parodic voice (that of Madame), tells her that for a maid she speaks too much. And, becoming once again the strong one, she forces Solange to re-enact the moment when the maid brings Madame her poisoned tea. Physically and spiritually dominated by Claire, Solange reluctantly complies. Claire drinks, and the curtain comes down as Solange, facing the audience, speaks the exultant speech of liberation: Madame is dead, she finds her own corpse as she returns home—that corpse from which have risen the freed and joyous maids.

Inasmuch as it exists at all, this is the physical level of the play, the part with which Genet is not truly concerned. It may indicate the lineaments of its action, but it fails to account for the protagonists, their circumstances, or the climate in which they move about. It does not even describe them. Who are these "maids"? At the level closest to reality, they are actresses playing a role which Genet has written for them. But that is precisely what Genet does not want. In the preface to the play, he complains that "the occidental actor does not try to become a symbol laden with symbols; he wants merely to identify himself with a char-

acter." A genuine maid on a stage would not be a stage-
worthy person: the quality of her presence would not make
of the stage a significant moment in the consciousness of an
onlooker. If an actress—not a maid—plays a maid and if
her "play" is to be more than the mere exhibition of what
a maid might be off stage, the quality of this new maid
(the actress-as-maid) must be derived in part from the
spectator's inability to dismiss her presence with the statement, "She is a maid." Instead, she is a hybrid, part actress,
part maid. As an actress, she is the half-goddess, the remote
creature of beauty and of luxury, the emanation of the mul-
tiple desires of those who see her as such and inform her
with their longing. On stage, she is more—she is the flesh-
and-blood creature, a woman to whom a spectator (or a
spectatress), also of flesh and blood, will respond through
animal calling. Her impersonation of the maid is going to
awaken a complex response in the spectator. A part of him
goes out to the creature of his dreams, the star; another
reaches to the woman, the scented and pulsating reality
before him; a third is being drawn into the words and
action upon which the character "maid" leaves her impress.
The author, the director who believes that it is this last
form of the "maid" who provides the most important of
these stimuli, will subdue the star and the woman (to the
extent that she is something besides a maid). Genet's intention is different. Maids exist outside the theater; so do
women—and even actresses (though to a lesser extent, since
their world carries forever with it at least a part of the
stage). But only in the theater are these several realities
blended within the irreality of the stage. It is the *stage* that
Genet wants to preserve, a justified bias that defines an art
form in terms of its ability to do what no other form can do
as well, as totally, or in the same way.

It is the quality "actress" that Genet wishes to emphasize,

not the quality "maid." These will thus be actresses acting—not actresses enacting maids, as this would start a descending line away from the theatrical illusion. They are playing at being, in an ascending line, maids who are in fact actresses and maids who think of themselves as actresses "laden with symbols," only the first of which is the inverted social order which they "represent."

The actress who plays at being a maid justifies one part of her being—she is a woman playing a woman. The tension provided by the equivocal actress-woman-maid breaks down at the point where "woman" and "maid" fuse. Genet has required for this play that the tension be carried forward along another upward spiral: the two maids are to be played by two young boys. Now the actor cannot identify himself immediately with any part of his creation. Or can he? For the ambiguity of the stage does not confine itself to the relation of the actor to his role; there is still another point of view represented by the spectator, a part of whom responds to the physical truth of an animal like himself, whatever its role and attributes. And the maids, young boys disguised as women, are acting out a strange, inverted relationship that involves the spectator directly in this stifling hothouse of flowers, phantasms, and the pomp of a weird ceremony.

The relationship of the maids is homosexual; is not a homosexual someone consciously enacting a role? The dress which each maid wears is part of an inverted sex-play which is not confined to the unreal stage, for beyond that stage the participant actors and spectators have been directly contaminated. But then, are these two figures? They are "sisters," they look alike to the extent that they can exchange roles—the homosexual polarity requiring two similar partners. Up to a point they are indeed distinct. Claire, the luminous one, incarnates the esthetic half of the homosexual act; she is the female principle within the male. Solange, the angel now in heaven, now fallen, is generally the male or destructive principle, the antiesthetic; she will destroy the symbol Claire. For a while, both performers are willing to conform to these parts. Solange is "in adoration" of Claire, and Claire acts the distant, detached, and desirable figure who is both the hierarchical and sexual mistress of Solange. She is haughty ("avoid touching me"), ironic, and cruel (Solange: "Madame is forgetting herself, Madame . . ."; Claire: "And what about your hands? Don't *you* forget your hands"), and these imperatives rouse the desire of Solange while confirming Claire in her role as an object of desire that is conscious of its empire.

But even as she is playing the role of the maid, Solange is drawn into the intensity of its significance and becomes the destroyer—the avenger of all servants, the immolating male. In those moments, the love relationship becomes one of hatred on the part of Solange who turns from active lover to executioner, while Claire, at that very same time, asserts the depth of her own meaning. She is beauty against which the slap of Solange and her hatred are unavailing; they can provide only a supplementary glow to her beauty: "Danger is my halo [. . .³]; and you, you dwell in darkness . . ." Thus, by merely extending in depth the significance of the principle which each symbolizes, the sexual and spiritual love that informs these principles turns into reciprocal and bitter hatred.

At this point, the ritual is interrupted by the intrusion of the nonceremonial world, the ringing of the alarm clock, a reality principle brought into this fairy bedroom from

³ In the original: "Danger is a nimbus to me [who am] Claire," that is, radiant.

the scullery. Claire is now simply a tired maid who rejects the previous relationship ("Stop trying to dominate me"). A part of their previous life endures in this existence, however. Claire, as Madame, had taxed Solange with her vulgarity (the vulgarity of a maid playing at being a maid) and her animal odor—a sin against the daintiness of Claire, but also against their homosexual essence, since that odor is presumably the milkman's whom Solange has been seeing illicitly in their garret. Now, in the world from which the mask has been dropped, Solange picks up the accusation: ". . . If the milkman says indecent things to me, he does to you too. But you loved mingling. . . ." It is now Solange who accuses her sister of contaminating the ritual with the reality of their single being. But Claire, whose name is symbolic, remains the lucid one, and she rallies against her sister. If Solange accuses her of soiling the ritual with their sordid reality, she can contaminate the reality of even Solange with her own vision, making of Solange an equally guilty accomplice: "Even in the garret, amidst all the [anonymous] letters [I was practice-writing to denounce Monsieur], you started swaying back and forth with [my] pitching." From this accusation, Solange can extricate herself only by asserting once again her destructive strength.

When Madame enters, the maids attain yet another dimension. In his analysis of Genet, Sartre says that when an actor comes on stage, he turns a previous reality into the irreality of a painted set and hollow props. But Madame is a catalyst of a different sort since it is she who enters as a prop, an artificial presence. She is a creature made up, dressed up, an actress playing the role of someone playing a woman of the world. She destroys the sumptuous apparatus of the maids: "Horrible gladioli, such a sickly pink, and mimosa! They probably hunt through the market before dawn to get them cheaper." But in so doing, she shows herself to be a coarser figure for having failed to enter into the ritualistic world of the maids. The maids are the aristocrats, and Madame is the plebeian symbol espousing only her single image; when she repeats the words that Solange had previously spoken in her stead, she sounds artificial, as if she were parodying the original. It is the maids who redeem the symbol of Madame by playing her part better than she does, by making her coarse reality a product of art. And this accounts for a part of the maids' hatred: the magnificence which they envy in Madame is of their (spiritual) making.

Madame's reality is likewise contingent. Part of her depends on the whims of her maids. Furthermore, as a false actress, she soon breaks down, abandoning her role while symbolically resigning her vestments to her handmaiden. That moment is brief (these moments are each limited— it never takes long for a present reality to be supplanted by another); Madame hears that Monsieur has been released, and she returns to her previous role. But she remains a lucid commentator of their reality: "Those girls worship me but [their performance] is the most extraordinary combination of luxury and filth." And she knows also the nature of their relationship: "You are quietly killing me with flowers and care. One day I'll be found dead beneath the roses."

The fatality of a symbol is its inevitable return to its fundamental meaning; whatever its changing forms, it has ultimately but a single revelation to make. That of Madame is to be Madame. She leaves the stage as she came on, unpoisoned—Solange says: "Didn't she drink it? (*Claire shakes her head* 'no.') Obviously. It was to be expected." Once she has left, the maids return to their ritualistic gestures and

the tensions that underlie them. Solange whips herself up
to a climax of destructive frenzy until Claire wilts, at which
moment the tenderness of Solange for her sister suddenly
wells up in her, and she compassionately leads Claire off
stage. When Solange returns, she speaks the soliloquy of
the murderess which the appearance of Claire, a few moments later, will dissipate. When in turn Claire forces
Solange to serve her the poisoned beverage, there is justification for wondering whether this gesture has any more
reality than the others. There is evidence to indicate that it
does not. Firstly, Claire, as Claire, is as weak as her sister:
she was the first to blurt out the news about the release of
Monsieur that ruined the attempted poisoning of Madame.
This attempted poisoning may well have been vain anyway,
since it is Solange who is supposed to have put the drug
in the tea and since she has already failed before to kill
Madame, captivated as she is regularly by the magnificent
aura of criminality—at the expense of the crime itself
("Incendiary! It's a splendid title!"). Even now, she has
failed to strangle Claire, preferring once again to the deed
the simulacrum, as in words she enacts the many steps of the
criminal's assumption. This is the final impotence of the
homosexual, his inability to do more than enact a ritual;
but this sham ceremony, the essential failure of the maids,
becomes a statement of their homosexual reality, sending
the play off again through this initial ambiguity into the
maze of its cross-reflecting mirrors.

The homosexual singleness of the two maids has already
been alluded to—they are in reality one. Solange says: "I
can't stand it any longer either. I can't stand our being so
alike, I can't stand my hands, my black stockings, my hair."
And the mirror image is echoed in Claire: "I'm sick of
seeing my image thrown back at me by a mirror, like a bad

smell. You're my bad smell." The entire ritual, their dialogue with its crises and its depressions, is a monologue, or, in Sartre's definition, the lonely and isolated sexual experience of the invert. Solange works herself up to a whiplashing climax or alternately thinks of Madame returning: "She'll cut the ground from under your fine adventure." The patterns of this drama are like the sterile turgescence and deflation of the homosexual act, conceived in loneliness and fraud and ending in deception. This is also the way in which each of Genet's plays is constructed.

If the ultimate significance of Madame is to be ultimately Madame, the actual mistress, the lesser reality of which the two maids will be the Platonic Idea, the ultimate significance of the maids is in their recurrent frustration, failure, and, withal, their comprehension of that which they cannot achieve. They exist only to perform a ritual that will never become more than just that. They have a sacred concept of their performance. "This room is not to be sullied" is one of the first injunctions of the limpid Claire. The ritual cannot be hurried without derogation. "Don't hurry, we've plenty of time," says Claire, while in fact, as she will indicate in her next breath, "Quick. Time presses." The chief concern of this ritual is that it be beautiful; it is played amidst flowers, with jewels and lavish ornaments, before mirrors, under the splendid light of invisible candelabra. ("You don't expect us [. . .] to organize things in the dark?" asks Solange, while at another time she turns the lights out to signify the end of the play within the play; still later, Claire tells her to light them up again, because the moment is too beautiful.) The language of its vulgar performers becomes lyrical and stately when the ritual calls for it. Genet, a latter-day Lyly, writes his ceremonial as a *Euphues* for the feminine ears of its performers, an elegant and harmonious prose whose illustrations are appropriately drawn from his own mythology and "unnatural natural history."

The purpose of the ritual killing that stands at the center of this drama is twofold. Death is first a form of splendor. Solange genuinely loves Claire, as her alter ego, as an embodiment of beauty, and in her role as the male immolator. Therefore, her words to Claire that confess her desire to murder her are significant: "I wanted to free you. I couldn't bear it any longer. It made me suffocate to see you suffocating, to see you turning red and green, rotting away in that woman's bitter-sweetness. Blame me for it, you're right. I loved you too much." Solange does not want to free Claire romantically from the clutches of her mistress, but to give her, with death, a splendor that will elevate her above her mistress, that will allow her a conclusive triumph. Love *is* murder to the homosexual (and perhaps it can be no more than that to anyone); it is the absorption by the lover of the loved one. Solange wants to possess Claire both as an act of assertive love and as one of selfless charity. Both demand the immolation of their victim; good taste and sensitivity require that it be a splendid immolation. But why, then, is there only a play-murder in this play? Here again, the answer lies in the esthetic concern of the maids, and to them is added still another dimension: they are the ordainers and the officiants of the dramatic act, the esthetic commentary. As the high priestesses of a rigorous ceremonial, it is the job of these Pythias to render audible the voice of a god. There is no evidence that Apollo ever appeared at Delphi; he merely spoke through the mouth of his handmaiden. And the god-stricken onlooker believed the pythoness because he knew her to be Apollo's handmaiden. The symbol of sacredness is not required to create, but merely to convince. The maids, no more than the theater, need produce the corpse of their victim. Their responsibility is only to make the spectator feel that he has witnessed a murder in that he felt the splendor of the act and thrilled to its mystery. For this to happen, the ritual must remain sterile. The reality of a corpse turns the play away from ritual as the spectator moves from awe to identification, as the mystery of an act becomes the reality of that corpse. Horror unalloyed must not be allowed to replace the more subtle feeling that blends with horror the image of beauty and the stirring of a singular experience. That is why the maids fail, why Solange is carried away from her homicidal act into the dream of homicidal magnificence. That is why it is also safe to assume that the climactic moment when the curtain comes down on Claire drinking the poisoned tea is a murder performed only in the spectator's intimation of it, but no more real for its priestesses than were any of their previous gestures.

In the chronological order of performance, *Deathwatch*[4] (1949) is Genet's second play. The scene, a prison cell, and its three performers recall Sartre's *No Exit* and that play's comment, "Hell is the others." But whereas in the play by Sartre each person exists as a witness to the incompletion of the others and exercises his destruction as part of a cooperative set of constants, each executioner is an independent and fluctuating quantity in the play by Genet.

The three characters (as well as the guard) are symbols and exemplars of beauty. They are there to provide, once again, an esthetic commentary. The center of attraction (Madame, in *The Maids*) is a convict named Green-Eyes,

[4] *Deathwatch* appears in *The Maids and Deathwatch* by Jean Genet, translated from the French by Bernard Frechtman, published by Grove Press, Inc., Copyright © 1954 by Bernard Frechtman. Quotations in subsequent pages are from this translation.

soon to be tried for the murder of a girl. Feeding each in his own way on the reality of Green-Eyes are two petty convicts, Maurice, a good-looking and impudent young hoodlum, and Lefranc, the literate outcast who writes Green-Eyes' letters to his girl. As in *The Maids* there is an absent catalyst who belongs to the gravitational center; the one who was Monsieur is here a Negro convict in another cell, Snowball. He is an exotic symbol: "He's black but he lights all ten thousand [prison cells of France]." Little is known about him beyond a romantic allusion to the robbery of a gold train.

Green-Eyes is the same curious hybrid as Madame: he is he-who-is. He has killed, or rather, a part of him has killed while another part of him stirs restlessly under the onus: "I ran right and left. I squirmed. I tried every shape so as not to be a murderer. Tried to be a dog, a cat, a horse, a tiger, a table, a stone!" And he dances a spiral-shaped dance in a vain attempt to move out of his present reality back through time. He is also strangely depressed at the thought that his woman will have nothing more to do with him; her dereliction confirms his sentence, his incontrovertible lonesomeness. But while experiencing the same fluctuations as Madame, he is also conscious at times of his splendor, of the loftiness of his isolation: "Who that's as young as me, as good-looking as me, has had the kind of tough break that *I've* had? I say 'the day of the crime!' That day!" And in these moments of exaltation, he is able to see other contingencies as pettiness, even to the extent of giving away his woman, over whose loss he had so grieved.

His ally is the hoodlum Maurice, an intelligent observer able to see accurately what is happening, although the reasons for the event often escape him. The keenness of Maurice derives in part from his admiration for Green-Eyes. To him, it is clear that Lefranc is falsifying the letters he writes for Green-Eyes and subverting completely the outer world of Green-Eyes. Maurice and Lefranc are set against each other: the play opens as Green-Eyes separates them, Lefranc having nearly killed Maurice in one of their periodic fights. The character and motivations of Lefranc are not immediately clear because the significance of certain of his actions is not immediately elucidated. He is a curious figure who has about his wrists and ankles the chain marks of the galley slave—a prestige among prisoners. He is as sensitive as Maurice to the aura of Green-Eyes. But he also holds up Snowball as a figure of even greater ascendancy. He purposely exchanges jackets with Green-Eyes and causes the latter to put on his own by mistake when Green-Eyes leaves the cell to talk to his wife during visiting hours. Lefranc's anger at Maurice, apparent from the moment of the curtain rise, does not prevent him from sharing his food with the young boy and, while Maurice is sleeping, from giving him his own cover. Aware of this, Maurice refers cynically to the actions of Lefranc and taunts him with the assurance that they cannot weaken the bond between him and Green-Eyes.

Lefranc is in fact an isolated figure. However, in this game of musical chairs, the shape of the triangle is forever changing. Green-Eyes relies on Lefranc for his letter writing even though he is aware of Lefranc's betrayal; he is detached from his wife but unwilling to sever the relationship that Lefranc provides him with through the words and phrases of letters that he cannot compose or the drawing of flowers that he cannot fashion. Moreover, a similar suffering, the maturity of these two criminals, gives Lefranc a proximity to Green-Eyes that Maurice with his youth, charm, and impudence cannot achieve.

Still, the isolated one is Lefranc. His literacy assumes a new meaning, an awareness of the criminals' significance and a will to preserve that significance. It is because of this desire that Lefranc has attempted to isolate Green-Eyes, to preserve him from the outer world whose bourgeois normalcy can only dim the splendor of Green-Eyes. More perceptive than the latter, more aware of his own singleness and luster, more willing to live by it, Lefranc not only has tried to cut off Green-Eyes from the unsanctified world beyond the prison walls, but has tried as well to make of the insiders a single unit, extending his protection to Maurice, claiming the aura of Snowball, exchanging his clothes with Green-Eyes', as once Claire had urged Solange: "Mix your muck with mine. Mix it! Mix your rags with my tatters! Mix it all up. It'll stink of the maids." But for Lefranc, the unity of the cell, of the entire prison, as an expression not only of their defiance but of their superiority to those who have excluded them.

At the level of his own concerns, however, Lefranc is just a petty thief "without class," as Maurice tells him. He is in fact attempting to steal Green-Eyes' personality (and Snowball's, and perhaps the beauty of Maurice). Green-Eyes is sublime because he is one of the elect—in spite of himself. The girl he strangled?—"It was fatality that took the form of my hands." He cannot formulate much about himself, barely enough not to tarnish his godliness. Lefranc, to whom this godliness has been denied, can do no more than formulate: his world is one of cerebration, that is to say, of fraud. And his love for the cell and its inmates is an attempt to achieve a sublime but fraudulent transmigration. When Green-Eyes is cut off from the world, Green-Eyes becomes a part of cell 108—the cell of which Lefranc is also a part. He also informs that aspect of Green-Eyes which is the jacket that he, Lefranc, puts on or the letters that he, Lefranc, writes; he gives those aspects of Green-Eyes his own being, his own imagination.

Lefranc experiences the temptation of the saint to live by his vision alone, to settle symbiotically upon Green-Eyes in a relationship that Genet calls "the eternal couple of the criminal and the saint" (in *The Maids*). Lefranc has the vision, not the reality; in reality, he is a fraud. In a world where tattoos are worn as a mark of distinction, Lefranc has a chest decoration, but it is not even skin-deep. It is a pen drawing of a ship, under which is the name "The Avenger," whose sacred horror endures in the reality of three famous criminals who bear it. The fraudulence of Lefranc is inevitably driving him from myth to ultimate deed. Both he and Maurice now know that within the world of Green-Eyes, Maurice has become the surrogate for the thing of beauty once represented by a girl wearing in her hair the sprig of lilac that Green-Eyes used to carry between his teeth. It is that girl whose murder has led to Green-Eyes' internment. It is her murder that was the mark of his election and his fatality: the discovery of the sprig of lilac on the corpse gave him away. If Lefranc is to move into the aura of Green-Eyes, he must strangle Maurice; he must perform once again the sacrificial gesture upon the appointed victim. This he now does, and the play becomes a commentary on what happens when esthetic distance is not preserved. Green-Eyes is not a killer. He is an incarnation of his own fatality—greatness is as much a part of him as his beauty, his green eyes. He is simply a force, blind and selfish, with no allegiance but to that force. He has already turned away from his lover Maurice and from the one who "organizes" his greatness, Lefranc, in order to move back into the realm which he shares with Snowball, for the Negro is of his kind.

He is able to do so, because betrayal is meaningless to a symbol, and doubly meaningless in a world whose conventions are for the living and the lawful, for whom he is an outlaw and, moreover, a man about to die. Green-Eyes is therefore indignant at Lefranc's useless murder, at the crude manner by which he has attempted to force his way into the company of the fated. And Lefranc, still lucid, is compelled to acknowledge the legitimacy of Green-Eyes' indignation. As the final curtain drops, he comments, "I really am alone."

Like *The Maids*, this play begins again as soon as the curtain has come down for the last time. Lefranc was a fraud, and his final act cannot project him into the circle of the elect. But his failure confirms his isolation. And were not the fatality and the greatness of Green-Eyes his dereliction: "Who that's as young as me [. . .] has had the kind of tough break that *I've* had?" Green-Eyes rejected the crime that signified his sanctity; Lefranc assumes the crime that marks his ineradicably as an outcast. Is the curse on both not similar? However, the circular movement is internalized: no one performs the ritual within the ritual of the play. Also missing is the tangible evidence of a sacred object. The talisman around which revolves the ritual of the maids is tangible—Claire in her blood-red dress, the locus of the ceremony, the very figures of the performers. But *Deathwatch* is set in a prison devoid of objects, and the charm is internalized also. Green-Eyes loves lilac and is betrayed by the fatal flower: the sprig is his talisman. But there is no lilac in this cell, and Green-Eyes must provide a verbal description of his symbolism or rely on the drawings of Lefranc. Whereas a spoken play can develop without objects because it is not centered on the stage but within the sensitive fiber of the spectator, the play that relies on a magic object keeps the stage as an objective center of the spectator's attention. The talisman remains distinct from the spectator and cannot leave the stage without losing its efficacy. For the actor of such a stage to internalize the ritual object by merely speaking of it amounts to removing the very basis upon which the play rests, forcing internalization by the spectator of that whose power derives from its objective distance. In the baroque drama of Genet, *Deathwatch* is strangely stylized and relies on an espousal by the spectator of the characters. Therefore, in this theater of blood and death occurs one of its rare murders: it cannot construct the horrific puppet necessary for Genet's black art. Because they must be accepted as people rather than as significances, these beautiful and fatal murderers and their bloody and exotic deeds lack substance, and the dramatic experience evaporates in a redolent puff of sentimental expressions and incredible deeds.

The Balcony [5] had its premiere in London in 1957, but has been rewritten since; thus the author shows greater concern for his work than his statement had hitherto indicated (cf. the comments in his prose writing, in particular *The Thief's Journal*, and also in the preface to the Pauvert edition of *The Maids*, "written out of vanity but in boredom. I abandon it to the editor").[6] The balcony as *locus mirabilis* existed already in *The Maids*, listed by Solange with such attributes of luxury and ceremonial as draperies, carpets, and mirrors; and it is also upon a balcony that the same

[5] *The Balcony* by Jean Genet, translated by Bernard Frechtman, published by Grove Press, Inc., Copyright © 1958, 1960 by Bernard Frechtman. Quotations in subsequent pages are from this translation.

[6] One might cite as further evidence of the author's interest in the theater the fact that the first staging of *Deathwatch* was his own.

Solange reached her apotheosis while enacting the splendor
and the execution of the criminal. The balcony is a stage
upon Genet's stage, a place of sumptuousness, triumph, and
make-believe.

The Balcony is a conscious stage from the first. A luster
is lit above it at all times as a permanent beacon within the
changing action; it is reminiscent of the chandeliers that
Christian Bérard once hung over the set of the Jouvet-
directed *School for Wives* to recall the moment of the play
and its nature—salon entertainment in the grand manner of
Louis XIV's court. But this stage is also "The Grand Balcony [. . .] the most artful, yet the most decent house of
illusions." A house of illusions is the traditional French
name for a brothel, a place for the creation and enjoyment
of intimate fancies. In his introduction to the 1960 edition
of the play, Genet warns the spectator not to move into a
sterile circularity by making of the stage a scapegoat. No
problem, says Genet, should be resolved in the imaginary
realm, especially since the dramatic solution is an indistinct
part of the closed social structure. It is rather the play that
should bring its reality to the spectator. And so Genet has
placed a mirror on the right-hand wall of his set which
reflects an unmade bed that would be, if this stage room had
a normal extension, in the midst of the orchestra's spectators.
The playgoer does not enter into *The Balcony* with im-
punity—once the curtain is up, he *is in* a bawdyhouse.

But he is also in the theater. The set *appears* to represent
"a sacristy," formed by three folding screens of blood-red
cloth: The sacristy is where the priest puts on the holy
vestments, the alchemist's kitchen (in *The Maids*, the scullery was referred to as the sacristy). Note that the setting
merely appears to represent; this is a stage, not the real
thing. The spectator must not attempt to fool himself; if

he makes of this a real sacristy, it loses its virtues of staginess and mystery, and the wellspring of ritual turns into a dressing room. It is made of folded screens (the latest play of Genet to date is called *Folding Screens*), those tenuous walls that are suggestion, not substance. And finally, the set is blood red, the color of the sacrificial and the sexual acts—the sacred ritual of death and rebirth as life, or as beauty, according to its moment. (Once before, Genet used the color for Claire's regal vestment as she played Madame.)

The curtain rises on an actor dressed as a bishop—or rather, on an actor who is at once a bishop and an actor: he has the miter and cope of the first and the unmistakable cothurni of the second (they are twenty inches high). His make-up is overly visible. He is, quite properly, a bishop larger than life-size. Two other people are with him, a girl in a lace dressing gown and Irma, in a black tailored suit. Irma is the owner of the brothel; this is her world. Outside, there is another world of blood and death. The town is in the throes of a revolution; throughout the play, the rattle of gunfire will be heard. These two worlds, that of the brothel into which the spectator is immediately drawn and that other on the outside which the spectator must imagine, are also those of the actors in the several roles they are performing. The bishop himself is in a metamorphic moment; his vestments are about to be removed. It is the moment of settling accounts with Irma, but a part of him remains in the former world, the one in which he has confessed the penitent girl in the lace dressing gown. His truth depends on hers: has she committed the sins of which he has absolved her or not? (For what is a bishop if not a man who can understand the nature of sin and has power to absolve the sinner?) That essential reduction of the ecclesiastical function is so central to the actor's concern that he does not wish to be a bishop—such a desire would be incompatible with his calling. But then, does he not refuse that temptation merely in order to be truly a bishop? Likewise, his penitent is a mystery. Has she committed the sins which she confesses only for the sake of the play in which they are engaged? These victims will turn coquettes in a moment of cruelty and dominate the torturer by refusing to disclose their innermost identity, upon which that of the torturer depends.

But if it is assumed that she should have sinned, the act performed by the bishop is mired in an actual mud: his abstracted vision becomes contingent upon the realities of others. It is not easy to remain within the imaginary world. To complicate matters further, the brothel is not limited to the bishop's fancies. A scream is heard—does it come from the outside, the streets upon which death is real and meaningless, or is it a part of the ceremonials within this theater? There are thirty-eight salons in Irma's house . . .

As this first salon fades into the darkness of the wings, another appears. Its performers are a judge, a girl, and an executioner. The half-naked girl has been whipped by the executioner, for the judge must exact a confession from her. The whip marks on her back and her tears are real at one level of this ceremony; her nakedness is inescapable at any level. But within this dual reality, the actor playing the judge lapses into yet another role—he has never seen the girl before, and as a law-abiding citizen, he is worried briefly, wondering whether she is a minor. The enactment of fear due to a legal concern displaces for a moment another legal concern enacted at another level of reality. But when the actor assumes again his role as judge, it is in order to step out of character and turn commentator within the absolute reality of the spectator. He says to the audience

that the role of a judge would be unbearable if each judgment tampered, in fact, with a human life. Therefore he is
dead, and the girl he is judging is a mere effigy too.

When the judge returns to his role on the stage within
the stage, he comments upon the interdependence of the
trio (the same interdependence as in *The Maids* and, especially, *Deathwatch*); he discovers, as the bishop before him,
that if the girl refuses to be a figment of his imagination
(a thief in this case), his own reality dies. And once again,
this girl is a tantalizer (though not necessarily as part of her
professional duties) and evasive: "Who knows?" The turning stage carries them off halfway between two realities,
the girl refusing to define herself as the judge pleadingly
licks her feet. The same scene is next performed by a
general and his lady-horse, and last, more briefly, by a tramp
and his pretty slave-tamer for, as Irma says, even misery is
magnified here.

These are moments of illusion, a theater for the private
enjoyment of certain people on stage who are not so very
different from the spectator—that participant watching the
proceedings from behind a peephole that has the full dimensions of the proscenium. The half-naked girls in the sadistic
sex play are exhibited to the spectator as well as to the
actor in his role as brothel customer—bishop, judge, general,
and so on. The world which these create in the stage privacy
of their own mind is just as much the spectator's; the objective stimuli are the same.

To this dimension which incriminates him, the spectator
is asked to add another for which the evidence is less explicit: it is that of the revolution echoed in the gunfire and
the concerns of the principals on stage. The contaminated
spectator participates immediately in only one level of the
actor's reality, for the actor on stage plays a role concerned

with events other than merely those of the brothel. Irma, at her cash register, wonders what will happen if the revolution should break through to her closed world. She will be killed, she will enjoy the sumptuous climax. At this moment, the spectator must effect a different translation, guided perhaps by the same Irma telling Carmen, the ex-prostitute who now keeps her books, to retain within her only the imaginary form of her little girl: "Dead or alive, your daughter is dead. Think of the charming grave, adorned with daisies and artificial wreaths, at the far end of the garden . . . and that garden [is] in your heart, where you'll be able to look after it . . ."

Against the intrusion of the revolutionaries, Irma has a powerful protector—the chief of police. He is a reality principle, existing as he does only in action: no one has ever asked to play his part in the house of illusions—to his irritation and dismay. But a reality principle cannot be the result of mere reflections since it is only its *doing*. Irma guards with vigilance the virtue of her creatures of illusion against such a moment as they—or others—might be tempted to change the illusion into substance. She frowns on even a hint of romance in these solemn rites of the flesh; she once had to kick out a mechanic for a related reason: "What with tightening screws, he'd have ended by constructing a machine. And it might have worked. Back to the [machine shop]!" Fact and fancy cannot be reconciled, and the Balcony is preserved in the distance which it maintains between its dreamers and those who act out the gestures of their dream. Still, the chief of police has a great yearning to be perpetuated as illusion, and he confuses the image of what he wants to be, an even greater incarnation of himself, with what he is, someone defined in action.

Genet now contrasts with the sealed world of the Balcony

the world of the revolutionaries. These are by definition
the ones who don't play; they are, like the chief of police,
the reality of their action. The brothel is their symbolic
enemy since its life principle—esthetic distance that separates the performer from his act—would be their death;
for them, "hand-to-hand fighting eliminates distance." These
priests of factuality are solemn. The danger to their revolution does not come from want of strength; it comes from
lack of purity. The moment their solemnity is in doubt, the
moment their action takes on the appearance of a game, they
will find themselves defeated even in victory, having merely
replaced the old order by another image of itself. Theirs is
the struggle of the purposeful against the purposeless; when
they have won, they will *organize* their freedom and their
relaxation, their festivities and their ritual. Their greatest
victory has been won not in the streets but through con-
version: one of the revolutionary leaders, Roger, has
brought over to their side a prostitute from the Balcony—
the singer Chantal. And it is out of that victory that defeat
will spread to the revolutionary camp. Chantal becomes the
illusion which even the revolutionaries now require in the
fire of action, the myth—a symbol singing on the barricades.
The revolutionary image must die, confused with the image
of that against which it was directed, in order for the revolution to succeed.

As the revolution gains, the brothel is partially destroyed
and is now a mixture of illusion and the outer reality. The
executioner, who was to have played a corpse later in the
evening, is now a genuine cadaver, felled by a stray bullet:

THE ENVOY: Yes, this body would have sent our dear Minister into raptures.

IRMA: Not at all, your Excellency. It's make-believe that
these gentlemen want. The Minister desired a

fake corpse. But this one is real. Look at it: it's
truer than life. His entire being was speeding towards immobility.

Against the spreading revolution that has destroyed the
palace and most symbols of power, the royal envoy draws
on Irma's bag of tricks: if the Queen is dead, whose reality
was evident only in absence and abstraction, then long live
the Queen in the illusion of her which Irma can provide.
Irma needs but organize her last illusion—to become herself the Queen, to withdraw into the absence of a virtual
death from which her subjects will derive the reality of her
presence. So real will she then become that when at last she
dies in fact, a worthless corpse will detach itself like a dead
skin from the imperishable idea. The other symbols of
power, the bishop, the judge, the general—the customers
trapped in the brothel—will assume the reality of their
vision which will now be confirmed by the reality of others
so that around the figment of the Queen might rise again
the pillars of authority.[7] The revolution is twice doomed:
first, in that its purpose was lost when it required the illusion
of Chantal in order to succeed; second, in its failure to
dispel the power of illusion of the figureheads, since a figment can be destroyed only by its creator.

Meanwhile in the brothel, the new seat of government,

[7] A consideration of the consummate way in which these actors
assume their parts compels one's attention to turn again to the
parts of the play that overlap the stage. Where did Genet, a convict and a vagrant since the age of ten, acquire the regal language
that is just as much a mantle for these heads of state as are their
other vestments? Is it not that in the midst of prison cells and
courts of miracles Genet was enacting the same private ritual,
playing for his own benefit (and self-protection?) the role of the
regal or divine figure disguised as an outlaw? Is not his whole
dramaturgy simply transcription?

the figures of temporal and spiritual power are rising against the Queen because their roles depend on others now, rather than on Irma. Either they *are* the power which they symbolize and which the populace confirms, or they return to the position which they first occupied on this stage—the private illusion which their Queen allows them. It is at this point that Chantal completes her final transmigration: she has perished in the collapse of the revolution—she has vanished as a symbol of illusion and has acquired instead the tangible reality of the corpse—even as the executioner. The symbolic weakness of the revolution has become, in death, an instance of its objective nature, an assertion of the realities with which it is able to cope. But this has happened too late for Roger, the defeated revolutionary who had brought Chantal over to his side. Roger, who has lost his purpose with the collapse of the revolution, comes to the brothel and, actionless, is the first customer who wishes to incarnate the symbol of action, the chief of police. The real chief of police who is watching this transformation is beside himself with joy—even though the others, who are more lucid, understand the meaning of what is about to happen. Symbolically sterile, Roger castrates himself while the chief of police is drawn into the impotent vision of his own projection. He disappears into the ideal image of himself, useless henceforth against a resurgent revolution whose illusion, Chantal, has been rubbed out so that once again it derives its strength from the actual world. As the machine guns again sound outside, Irma puts out one by one the lights in a now functionless brothel, leaving only the lamp-lit image of the sterile chief of police, the imagination of Roger within which the chief of police has achieved his ideal reality.

The Balcony is largely an expository play, a commentary

upon the nature of reality and illusion and upon the function of the stage. *The Blacks*,[8] first performed in 1959, is the play based on that theory. In *The Balcony*, the royal envoy had said of one of the figures about to assume the symbolic shape of power, "Hurry. I'm wasting my time listening to your nonsense. [. . .] If that gentleman will not do, find a dummy, but hurry" (end of the seventh tableau, in French text only). In *The Blacks*, Genet demands a public of whites. He is insistent upon this to the extent of asking for at least one ceremonial white spectator if the play were performed for an audience of blacks, in which case the entire performance would be addressed to that single figure. Lacking even that single sacrifice, the blacks would have to wear white masks. "And if the blacks refuse the masks, then a dummy will have to be used." Thus the magic object has now moved beyond the footlights into the hitherto privileged realm of the spectator. This play forces implementation of Genet's admonition: "Let no problem be resolved in the imaginary world."

The stage of Genet is more important than the spectator since it requires a specific spectator and, barring that, a spectator disguised. (If the stage should have to settle for a dummy white, Genet will have succeeded in inverting completely the order of things: the performers will then be playing for only themselves.) The play is first of all a game, a diversion whose full meaning will be made clear later on; on stage, it is a performance put on by blacks for the benefit of other blacks dressed and masked as whites. It will be, as conceived by blacks, a definition of blacks by whites for the benefit of an exclusively white audience. Its

[8] *The Blacks* by Jean Genet, translated from the French by Bernard Frechtman, published by Grove Press, Inc., Copyright © 1960 by Bernard Frechtman. Quotations in subsequent pages are from this translation.

paraphernalia will be the customary flowers and a coffin, the sacred objects in a ritual concerned with beauty and death.

Genet begins this act of play by eliminating the stage. The curtain does not come up mechanically, but is drawn —the human hand, portent of human mystery, replaces the machine. Thereafter, Genet adds the aspect of reality that ultimately defiles the mystery of the figureheads in *The Balcony* by making the reality of their first vision dependent upon the vision of someone else: these blacks are played by Negroes. At this level of reality, the spectator cannot detach himself from the stage. At the time the play, after some delay, was finally staged in Paris, voodoo troupes were offering, on other Parisian stages, experiences ranging from tribal dancing to what purported to be the genuine trances of the voodoo curse. What Genet proposes with *The Blacks* is, by means of an artifact, to project the spectator into a world of mystery and magic that will affect him more surely and more intensely than even the voodoo ritual.

Having stated the primacy of the stage-as-reality, Genet proceeds to subvert that reality in order to make of the stage the place of magic and mystery which it must also be if it is to sustain a genuine ritual; something is going on somewhere beyond this stage—an emissary occasionally breaks into the play with news from a world alien to the one of the play. The pseudo-whites on the dais are obviously actors, and not very good ones. Those who are below, performing for them, although they are ostensibly actors and spectators in a yet unspecified ritual are likewise learning their parts as actors and spectators. On each of these levels, the actual reality is being transformed into an artifact— something which will acquire a dimension other that that of its immediacy as existence.

The "whites" upstairs have come to witness the ritual murder of one of their number. The "organizer," who is a central performer in every one of Genet's plays, is a black by the name of Archibald, and he begins the ritual. This is built around a catafalque on center stage which supposedly contains the remains of a white savagely murdered by the blacks. The play is defined by Archibald as ritual: tonight again, the play goes on, the scene is to be enacted once again. The theater is asserting its own reality; these blacks are *ideas* of blacks—white pictures interpreted by the blacks themselves. Although they are Negroes, they now exist at their own level of the stage. In addition to being the generic reprobates, the outcasts that people each of Genet's stages, they are the shoeshine blacks, bad-smelling, lustful, murderous, childish—and, withal, exotic symbols because of these nonwhite attributes and because of their physical power and beauty. The whites are similarly mental images, though less complex. They are the black's notion of white authority, a Queen with her court around her, the church, the army, the flunkies. These "whites" try to see themselves as a necessary radiance; they are the born masters whose being legislates and justifies. The blacks, in addition to their own definition of themselves, are able to legitimate their personal feelings by this view of the "whites": their "black" hatred, their desire to possess and kill, rape, and obliterate those who need not justify their own rule over them, returns the stage gradually to the reality of that which encompasses even the stage. Genet is transferring to these blacks the prerogatives of the criminals, the perverts, and the inverts of his plays and novels. They are automatic forces attempting to become more consciously and more hugely *themselves,* in order to "deserve [the whites'] reprobation, [to merit] the judgment that will condemn";

otherwise life deals too cruelly with the fated outlaw.

It is thus for the blacks to analyze what they are—the negative of a positive image. The black named Village once loved the black girl Virtue: "When I beheld you, suddenly —for perhaps a second—I had the strength to reject everything that wasn't you, and laugh at the illusion" (Beckett's Henry, in *Embers*, as the roaring waves briefly remember him). But he "was unable to bear the weight of the world's condemnation" and began to hate her. Archibald spells out the inanity of the word "love" for Village who is both an actor in a play and a black, that is to say, the fated actor in the larger play of his daily existence: neither can speak of love, the first because of the illusoriness of his being, the second because his being is defined for him by the whites. Village wants to escape from this play into reality, but Archibald points to the white audience: there is no exit.

Their ritual is not arbitrary; it has evolved through many trials and repetitions. It is both necessary and resisted still by those who are not fully convinced. The deacon, for example, is blind to the game that defines the warring participants, because of his belief in a transcendental principle. If the game must be played nevertheless, he would like to preserve merely the esthetics of the ritual, to make of *The Blacks* a play without the reality of its topical reference. The several realities of these actors are sometimes strikingly reminiscent of the independence that Brecht wished for his own.

The ritualistic killing which the blacks will now enact (for what is in the coffin is of little importance, "an old horse will do, or a dog or a doll"), that symbolic gesture, must thus not only destroy an individual, aiming at the destruction of a historical moment, but also the mask which that individual wears—the black hatred worn by the white.

These endless interreflections of murder (for "This is the theater, not the street. The theater, and drama, and crime") encompass not only the symbolic coffin and the stage play in which Village repeats his murder born of the desire and hatred of a white girl, but they catch up as well the entirety of the stage whose reality becomes a magical object within the actuality of the spectator's existence.

This grisly tribal dance of passion and murder is suddenly broken short by Genet; the esthetic and voodoo object is cast aside. News comes from the outside which all the blacks gather about to hear, including those on the dais who remove their false white faces. The emissary, who had already interrupted that action previously, has news at present that is unambiguous. A congress has elected the one who is on his way to organize the fight: "Our aim is not only to corrode and dissolve the idea they'd like us to have of them, we must also fight them in their actual persons, in their flesh and blood." The Negroes on stage were real as "blacks," not as actors in their various roles. Now Genet actualizes even the roles which they were playing. Not only were the blacks representing to the symbolic whites on the dais the metaphor of an off-stage reality, but it turns out that the real plot is being performed beyond the theater. Blacks are rising the world over (the white spectator need only recall what he read in his afternoon newspaper before entering the theater), while these blacks on stage were providing a screen with their ritualistic actions—actions which were in part the beauty demanded by the deacon but were also a topical exercise performed within the microcosm of the theater, with whites drowsing in the illusion of a play as blacks rise to action before their sinking figures.

There remains only for the play to close, anticlimatically (and so to justify its caption, "Clown show"): grotesquely, the blacks kill off the puppets of power who have once more put on their white masks. Only a passing thought by the "white" Queen, as she is about to die, sends this circular play into its final, cosmic orbit. As an actress whose role is to perform a ceremonial descent into death, she wonders about the day, maybe a thousand years hence, when, long after tables have been turned and the blacks have eroded themselves into their own doom, she in turn may arise again and play over the ritual as a white. Meanwhile, in another world, Village can once again love Virtue since the play is over. The curtain falls. But if Village can love Virtue, is it not because he and she have assumed their blackness? And if they are black, is there not a white eye to see them as blacks and will they not again have to move into the vision of that white eye, existing according to its vision?

This drama is fraudulent. The white spectator (any spectator) who has seen *The Blacks*, or any play by Genet, has been deceived. He has seen a conjurer, or what Sartre calls an elegant ballet which is the orchestration of those interreflecting mirrors. At the moment of his most intense perception, that which he derives from the human revelation of the magical object, he has been concerned with only a small part of man, the part giving the illusion status as an essential human perplexity. But the human perplexity is far more complex. Man does not live by any single anguish —nor, incidentally, by the raptures of an esthetic experience. As on the stage of Brecht, a single fiber, however vibrant, does not define man.

Genet's latest play in 1961, *Folding Screens* [9] (*Les Paravents*), unhappily confirms these strictures, while confirming also the great gifts of a dramatist whose scenic

---

[9] To be published by Grove Press, Inc., as *The Screens*, translated by Bernard Frechtman.

expression finds new and imaginative terms in each succeeding play. *Screens* is the leisurely chronicle in seventeen scenes of the customary outcasts of Genet on their way to oblivion. This time, the outcasts are a normal couple, man and wife, the Arabs Leïla and Saïd, outcasts in the homosexual's view. Their isolation assumes many forms. They are ugly, as only Genet can portray ugliness, with its physical horror, its stench, its vulgarity (the euphemism of Leïla's hideousness is the one-eyed hood she wears). Like the Negroes in *The Blacks*, the Arabs are outcasts within a world dominated by another race, and as in *The Blacks* again, they are at war with their foreign overlords. For their isolation to be absolute, these outcasts turn traitors to their own kind (following a pattern already noted in *Deathwatch*) so as to remain isolated even within the world of the outcast. And in a hallucinatory ending, the very dead are seen waiting for this damned couple in vain: their death is an extinction beyond even the power of death to conceive.

Genet has woven this chronicle into the reality of present events, in a setting which is presumably Algeria. He has provided a lush fauna of whores with their traditional ritualistic dignity and the heavy burden of sacred isolation (symbolized by their heavy brocade skirts that are weighted down with lead); caricatural *colons* (the white landlords, similar to the caricatures performing on the dais of *The Blacks*); and soldiers, whose ritual of sex and savagery makes of them yet other exemplars of a total exclusion associated with what Genet praises most—beauty, evil, splendid remoteness, the qualities of purity and election that denote his saints.

The themes are old. What is fresh is Genet's scenic imagination. Significantly, the play is not named for the people or its action, but for its props. The screens are the objects which the dramatist has placed upon this "open-air theater" whose floor is an "earth platform." "In contrast with the objects drawn as realistic still-life on each screen, there must always be on stage one or more real objects." These are the two levels of the stage, its reality and its irreality, upon which each of Genet's plays is a commentary. The screens are the manifest irreality of the stage. Its people and its tangible props are its symbolic reality, for they are to be transformed by the irreality of the stage, just as the screens are to bring to life the imaginative reality of the play.

In this play whose actors play many roles ("each actor will be obliged to play the parts of five or six people, men or women"), the reality of the human being can be little more than symbolic. "*The characters:* If possible, they will be masked. Otherwise, they should be heavily painted, heavily made up (even the soldiers). Excessive make-up to contrast with the realism of the costumes." And as the living part of the stage is thus transformed into its ritualistic object, its backdrops become the imaginative dream that is alive with the reality of the spectator. On a stage whose actors play the sounds of animals, of the wind, of rain—thus lending their immanence to that which cannot objectify its own—the reality of the actor also fades alongside that of the screens. Upon these, incendiaries light their multiplying fires (each painting his "yellow flame" upon a screen which seems transformed into a roaring conflagration), others bring in their loot (each drawing his item of booty so that the screens are covered with them and give the stage the appearance of a junk shop); upon them too, seasons come and wane, constellations appear, life ebbs and flows. In a similar way the physically real people give up their corporeality in order to create the wind and the rain, their bodies and their manner responding to the reality of non-existent elements. Thus Saïd's mother creates the tree to which she is talking, through gestures that convey the Platonic Idea of an otherwise invisible tree.

This is the area of Genet's mastery: the ritual which is the stage performance, the reality derived from its objects, the sacredness conferred by that stage upon its objects and its people, so that their former being outside the magic circle of the stage is transcended. The image is of course hollow. But in addition to the hollow image which Genet demands, since the ritual starts with a fetish, there is a great hollowness at the center of his drama. In "The Criminal Child," Genet speaks of his love of Nazi horror camps. His "envy" of their suffering is disproportionate, however, because he has shown himself incapable of assuming either the imaginary "crimes" of those tortured or their innocence. He is naïvely juxtaposing the pin in the voodoo doll and the beast-inflicted torture, confusing the automatic criminal (whose automatism is no better than that of the bourgeois) with the slaughtered innocent; there is little in common between the mechanical acts of the first and the imposed suffering of the second. Genet's very saintliness—the rigor involved in remaining a criminal—constitutes a dereliction of freedom that bears too great a resemblance to the dereliction of others whose objectives are less admirable: both are equally illegitimate in the long run. There are other ways to beauty.

The magic of his stage holds the spectator under its spell for the duration of the performance. But on reflection, the absolute assertion of a force greater than man is sterile because there is nothing with which to compare the absolute assertion. Such reflections are outside the realm of the theater, however. Within it, no one has yet so magnificently duped an audience, and there is no playwright writing today who is more legitimately possessed of the theater.

V ~ POSTSCRIPT

THE difficulties of existence expressed by these four authors are dissimilar and suppose different consequences in the theater. For Brecht and Genet, the problem is technical rather than metaphysical, even though the whole life of Genet has been a *performance.* Brecht was a witness (for the prosecution) of his time; *The Expedient* is perhaps a central play in the work of Brecht because of its form and statement. The play is in fact an arraignment before a jury and judges: this is the climate and the form which Brecht wanted for all his drama. But in attempting to devise the conditions whereby the stage might become the rational courtroom, the place where argument and refutation are presented and weighed, Brecht came up against the reality of the theater which has a climate and a form of its own. Brecht's difficulties as a witness derive from the demands of the two worlds in which he wanted his testimony heard, those of the courtroom and of the stage. For the intellectual Brecht, this presented largely a technical problem; and as the result of thirty years' research, he left not only plays that are debatable evidence of his experimental success, but an impressive body of technical writing on every aspect of the dramatic performance that makes of him one of the foremost theorists of the contemporary theater.

At some point, the witness must discriminate. For Genet, the problem of the witness is more intimate than it is for Brecht. Existence is not a collective phenomenon for Genet. As Saint and Sinner, man and homosexual, aristocrat and thief, asserter and outcast, Genet has lived a double life, remaining consciously mask and marrow, ritualist and renegade. His single constancy was that of his double vision, the inherent self-consciousness that kept him at all times an actor. The effortlessness of his plays reflects his intimacy with every form of the dramatic ritual, antedating his very knowledge of the stage. And every one of his plays grows out of his personal need to define within the texture of being the warp and the woof that are reality and illusion.

The difficulties experienced by Ionesco and Beckett do not concern the stage. It is a nausea of existence that actuates Beckett: his playwriting is informed by the same revulsion that determines his prose writing—and presumably every vital act of his. And if Vladimir or Clov are merely Beckett himself borrowed for an evening by an actor with no stage existence of his own, the stage is not called into question. Beckett's existence expresses the agony of being unable to vanish, but it expresses nothing about the processes of the stage. The drama which he has created is merely another deception, another means of killing time (which, like all other things in his world, will not die).

Ionesco too makes an ontological claim in expressing the difficulty of living, and that claim supposes that his drama is merely a part of his inner trauma. Inasmuch as Ionesco begins as a subverter and a practical joker, he is certainly close to a form of personal expression; but the part of the stage that is sham and mask can legitimately support such fun. If, however, Ionesco believes in the moral extensions of this facetious protest, he gives up his claim to the stage as a physical object subverted and subverting. The immediacy of his tampering is lost; he is no longer creating a dramatic universe with his hands, but is moving off instead into the abstract realms of the theorist.

For Beckett, for Genet (and for Ionesco, if indeed the play is incidental to his life), the play is sacrificed—but only from their own viewpoint. When, as dramatists, they give

up their construct, its appropriation by the theater starts it through avatars which they can hardly control, for in the three-dimensional form which it acquires, the play is dependent for its depth on a double perception, and that perception is no longer wholly the author's as the spectator comes into being. The play in the theater is similar to the surrealists' mirror whose reflecting face does not prevent the poet from entering the world that lies beyond the surface reflection. Drama, in its performance, reflects an illusion of surfaces; yet all the while, its silvering is transparent and allows another world within the looking glass. The play, as it is performed, is but half of the experience referred to as "theater." The half that completes it is the spectator, whose reflection is upon the face of the mirror even as his being is drawn into it. The mirror held up to the spectator tells a story of surfaces, the interplay of epidermis and illusion. But the spectator is also allowed to move beyond the silvering and to enter a world whose dimensions and whose pulse are his.

The spectator is free. His only limits are those which his rational faculties impose upon him, but even these he is free to suspend. The looking glass is there for Alice to walk into. It is the critic who refuses to enter, dubbing her world fairyland or satire. All the world's a stage, until it is questioned: at that moment it reverts to mental speculation, to analyzable illusion.

When Alice moves into the looking glass, she encounters a number of creatures endowed with her reality, the Tiger-lily, the Red Queen, Tweedledum and Tweedledee, and so on. It is because of their reality that she exclaims: "O Tiger-lily [. . .] I *wish* you could talk!" It is the critic who replies: "We *can* talk [. . .] when there's anybody worth talking to."

There is little doubt that the theater was born real—as real as the sun, the stars, the storms, the laughter and the tears of man. The stage was a place of reality, that is to say, a place of abiding awe and mystery, since only that which resists complete explanation is able to retain its reality and its life. There is little doubt that for a very long time the god who came down from above to unravel the play was a genuine god. It is only much later that people became aware of the machine: the spectator was moving back from the stage—he was turning critic. Soon after, the gods disappeared altogether.

"Theater" is first a man in action in front of another man. The nature of his "action" and the form of his words are questions that arise outside the theater and subsequently. At the beginning, there is merely the act of a human being whose gesture binds to him another human being. This is true of all art, inasmuch as the term and its distance from the antonym are statements of a human experience and measurements proceeding from a human quantity. But in the dramatic experience, the human gesture is its own ultimate extension and can be apprehended immediately by the human participant (the misnamed "spectator") without the interposition of thought or artifact.

Only one instrument is equal to the complexity and the sensitivity of man; that instrument is the theater's own, the identical human being within the actor. The air breathed by the man on stage feeds the spectator alike; the depths of his sexual being are atune to those of the human being before him; his voice becomes a tactile link between flesh and flesh.

It is man viewed as the utmost dimension and the single principle of the dramatic event that enables Aristotle to see in tragedy the imitation of actions arousing pity and fear. Pity and fear are unreasoning emotions that well up from animal depths before the mind is allowed to assert the distance between *theatron* and *skene*. Fear, the visceral expression of the organism endangered, and pity, the awareness of one's hurt in a kindred hurt, are the immediate responses of a man instinct with the recognition of a man. In giving the stage expression of these emotions the name tragedy, Aristotle defines it as the most intimate likeness and the fullest expression of the reality principle (represented by the spectator) which the stage can attain.

Such a state of grace is rare. The participant in the tragic event, the tragic spectator, must be "pure." For Alice (if not for Lewis Carroll), the Tiger-lily, the Red Queen, Tweedledum and Tweedledee are cognate beings: it is not Alice who laughs. The dramatic ritual is likewise an act of faith accessible only to such as are utterly candid—that is to say, untainted. The dimensions of the stage instrument will suggest a proliferation of responses; no part of the spectator may dwell inert before the stimulus.[1] It will place before him utter nakedness; no self-consciousness must allow

[1] Ideally, the dramatic performance is *total;* it attempts to define the many complexities of a human being and requires therefore a *total* spectator to commit his substance to the dramatic illusion. This should reassure critics who have professed to see in these esthetics the banishment of the mind—the more so as it is not possible to speak of an exclusively visceral response any more than it is possible to speak of an exclusively mental one. Both are interdependent; at a certain point, both coexist. This analysis (in itself a wholly mental exercise) is concerned merely with questions of emphasis and proportion. It rejects the illegitimate appropriation by the mind, the process that stifles an animal response by examining its stimulus as if it were merely theoretical, as if that stimulus rather than its extension within the spectator were the object of the dramatic performance. Those who consciously play at being spectators are the ones who out of self-consciousness overextend the legitimate province of the mind; they are most likely the same ones who, outside the theater, play consciously at living.

him to veil his own. The tragic spectator must be an instrument attuned and open to the full pitch and temperament of the dramatic event.

Many have thought that a marionette ought to replace the actor; the names of Gaston Baty, Gordon Craig, Michel de Ghelderode, and Alfred Jarry come to mind. In the days of a waning theater, these were people concerned with its survival and determined to see it attain once more the dignity and the stature of man. Their protests were directed against an instrument debased, something less than man— the particularized actor of the commercial stage. They believed that the actor had become a limited instrument, skilled only in rendering tics and surfaces, whose presence mocked the human potential lost. They saw in the puppet meant to replace such objects the image of a "God" (Craig) or of a "superman" (Jarry), in whom no surface detail would cancel a deeper significance.

The temptation of the marionette is thus a temptation of the absolute: divinity and superman are aspirations of man seeking his own ultimate extension. His vision and his substance fill the theater, and the ultimate actor is the one who can best acquire the shape of that vision and that substance. Those who wanted a marionette instead of a man had hoped that the impassive puppet would merely efface every contingent detail that detracted from such an ultimate.

The presence of a man in the theater has long been considered one of its impurities by critics for whom drama remains within the purlieus of literature. The puritanical tradition has subscribed to this view because it ignores the sensual aspect of the stage (see Robert Nelson, *Play within a Play*); and the French, ever mindful of the Cartesian myth, have been especially ingenious in developing the idea to favor a mental theater (it is, for example, a frequent argument of André Gide; see also Paul Valéry, *Monsieur Teste,* Jean Hytier, *Les Arts de littérature,* and so on). Analyses of this sort establish a false analogy. Only an echo of drama occurs at the level of the mind; literature and drama are unlike. Literature may indeed propose the *mental* definition of a man, but in the theater, the compelling gesture of a man starts a *sensual* suasion. That gesture originates in depths that are at once more compelling and more intimate than the mental prefiguring. No intellectual process is either as immediate or as assertive as the flesh.

Nor are the actor's words to be confused with the words of literature. They too are flesh creating, and responding to, impulses that elicit identical life within the flesh of the spectator. The words of the man on stage cannot be confined to mental assimilation any more than the symphony can be *heard* (a complex and sensual operation) through a reading of its score. The act of speaking the word transforms it: it becomes part of a man.

Words are bivalent. One part of them names, the other suggests; one part asserts a fact, the other allows a fantasy; one part is didactic, the other musical. At one extreme, the word is an object; at the other, it is poetry. There is a form of literature that never leaves the printed page, for its statement brooks no intrusion. There is another that is insubstantial on paper and acquires definition only in the reader. The stage makes but a single assertion, that of the living presence; all other assertions start masking the reality of that presence. Therefore, to preserve the substantive reality of the actor and of the spectator, all other parts of the theater are insubstantial, and its words must remain music, suggestion, poetry.

In the introduction to an early play of his (*Les Mariés de la Tour Eiffel,* 1921), Jean Cocteau establishes a useful difference between "poetry *of* the theater" and "poetry *in* the theater." The theater has its own mode of expression which it can never achieve by simply transferring literature, however suggestive, *into* the theater. The dramatic suggestion remains of a different sort, tied as it is to the many dimensions necessary to weave the spectator into the dramatic texture. Cocteau's catchwords refer to much more than words.

Just as every other dramatic effort is subservient to its delineation of a man, so the stage endeavors to tell the story of a man—at least in its moments of aspiration. In its worst moments of sloth, the stage can never succeed in dismissing altogether the man that stands upon it. Therefore, the tragic shadow never quite lifts from the stage, even though it recedes as the spectator withdraws from the stage.

The tragic nature of man derives from the fact that his absolute vision is tied to an impotent expression. That vision frustrates the visionary who is grounded forever and forever doomed to hope for more than he can attain, to see more than he can grasp, to feel more than he can explain, to fear more than he can control. Until the vision is canceled out at last without ever having been achieved, the finite part of man pursues it in vain along an exasperating and vicious circle. Hopeless flights, inner torment, lingering frustration define the human condition. It sets man apart from the animal that does not question these limitations and equates him with God that sees beyond them. The tragic conflict is the one that rages within man, and since the postulate of pain dooms his mightiest efforts to dominate that pain, wherever man appears, there appears also the impress of tragedy, his inalienable sign. The onlooker or the participant may avert his sympathy and term man ridiculous: such a gesture merely signifies a personal need to escape temporarily from substance to surface. It is a momentary suspension of reflection rather than a statement about an inherent condition. Tragedy remains attached forever to some part of the theater.

This is not to say that the stage necessarily accepts its tragic implications. The downfall of the modern stage can be seen in the distance that separates gods from objects. The theater began with at least the immanence of gods, and long thereafter concerned itself exclusively with the god, or the god's power, in man. The mechanical props with which it continues to function are a recent development; they are not meant to satisfy the god in man.

The god in the spectator requires a god on stage—or at least heroes: Aristotle desires that tragedy imitate "men superior to reality." And indeed, tragedy is merely a trick that suggests an optimistic view of man; it tells *first* of man's limitations, but it ends in triumph. Out of the ruins, a greater man is born—even though this may be the moment of his physical death. Death, man's ultimate statement otherwise, becomes in tragedy the litotes that measures the greatness of his revelation. Bloody and blinded, Oedipus relies on an inner vision that shames the limited perception of the former man. The spectator may experience that triumph elsewhere, but only in the theater is he allowed to feel that this is an ultimate state not subject to the rip tides of limiting awareness. In *The World as Will and Idea*, Schopenhauer says that comedy must hasten to let the curtain fall so as to spare us what follows. The tragic curtain serves an identical purpose.

Gods and heroes are receptive only to the most essential suffering and joy of which man is capable; the spectator will not grant his being for less (and less is not worth granting). Gods and heroes are terribly vulnerable: a blackhead or a banana peel can kill them. They perform in an action whose overtones are far more portentous than is the action itself—the latter being merely the consequence of the former (the words are those of Louis Jouvet in *Témoignages sur le théâtre*, 1954). The spectator must readily accept that the action is a conventional symbol; the mirror must not remain opaque. If some opacity allows him to think that there is no more than the symbol, the spectator will remain on the surface of the drama. That surface must therefore be as solemn and as innocuous as possible—the puppet world of Craig and Baty, the myths of classical antiquity.

The more the drama demands a specific conditioning of the spectator, the less will be its scope, the more limited will be its appeal, the more quickly it will age, the less it will be able to justify itself. The myth is important only because of its unimportance. The critics who believe that Antigone can be understood only when the Sophoclean world is accepted (for example, Henri Gouhier, *Le Théâtre et l'existence*, 1952) would have to look upon any classical performance today as merely a scholarly exercise —and of course they do not. The myth never dies simply because no myth is ever alive, and so it endures concomitantly with the life that it enfolds: the spectator's responsive passions, pity and fear, to which might be added the states of man that are beyond man's power to alter, joy, sadness, anger, love. There are few of them.

It is only when a man becomes more interesting that the explanation of what makes him act that such response is possible. The hero and his fatality must be greater than the rational faculty to explain them away. If Jean Racine's *Phèdre* (1677) is not the Phaedra of old, possessed by the gods, but merely a clinical case, or even the searching of a Jansenist conscience, Phaedra becomes less terrible (in the Aristotelian sense) since a known quantity begins to limit her mystery and her freedom. From the standpoint of the tragic heroine, the precincts of medicine or of Jansenist morality are external and rigid; they cage the animal. And an animal caged loses, along with its threat, its reality: if the spectator is not in genuine danger, he is merely curious —the drama reverts to intellectual analysis. It is only when the will of the gods hounding Phaedra blends with the spectator's intimate knowledge of his own helplessness and when her stage terror is informed by his that Phaedra lives in his anxiety which no analysis or creed can relieve.

Modern authors have been reluctant to impose upon the spectator the stringency of tragedy. They have been wary of its vulnerable heroes; they have questioned the existence of a candid spectator. Having measured the distance between proscenium and public and satisfied themselves that the modern spectator is sedate and sedentary, they have not sought to draw him onto the stage. Nearly every form attempted by the modern stage admits at least an implicit separation between stage and spectator.

Even for the classical century of French drama, admiration is proposed as the key to the tragedies of Pierre Corneille by those who see in his drama the primacy of reason in a pre-Cartesian form. The spectator thus retains his autonomy, but his presence on stage is not required; he is asked only to marvel, that is to say, properly, to doubt. This theory, which is able to devise a wholly rational stage creature for whom the world is sealed and fully explainable, even as he is, devises a hero that remains external to the incompleteness of the spectator. Such a hero lacks the systaltic action that conditions the reality of the spectator —the alternating pulse of his transcendental vision and of his dejection. There is a second reason for which the curtain must fall on Oedipus triumphant. The fallible half that makes Oedipus a man is canceled by his epiphany; it is no longer possible for the spectator to hold intercourse with him.

As his actions do not proceed from an inherent necessity, the admirable hero (often the hero of the romantic stage) depends on a situation; his being is subservient to a coincidence not justified by human inherences. It is thus difficult for him to compel the allegiance of the spectator who is asked to accept a fraudulent world in which contingencies must be taken as absolutes. Tied to a historical set of determinants, that hero loses all purpose once the external and transitory agencies upon which his being depends have evolved and altered the circumstances from which he drew his substance.

In the art of seduction called theater, the living actor is not a *sine qua non*, but merely the most powerful and immediate of enticements. If the theater gives up the human lure in its courtship of man, it must try to ensnare the spectator in ways that leave him as much as possible to his own devices. The evocation of a man on a stage where there is none will be more than ever an act dependent on the good will and potentialities of the spectator.

Conditioning through publicity, common acceptation, music, and so on may awaken in the spectator a latency of response, a readiness to cast his reality into the shape which the stage will propose. Stage lighting is able to suggest mere lineaments and spectral worlds which the spectator may be willing to fill. Sets are usually designed for the same purpose, although their tangibility carries with it the temptation of coercion. If that temptation is indulged, the set will stress a single reality that may clash with, or impede, the spectator's. The slabs of raw beef on the naturalistic stage could not be more genuine; therefore, it was difficult for them to suggest more than might an actual butcher shop—hardly an organon equal to the possibilities of the theater.

The words which the actor is given to speak are another means of suasion. Like every stage stimulus, they may be absolute or programmatic, reminders to the spectator of his immanence or refractory embodiments of a single and limited assertion. The heroes of Corneille speak Alexandrine verse, and sometimes that verse is sublime. Alexandrine verse indicates a desire to transcend everyday life. If that verse is also genuine poetry, that is to say, a human utterance whose depths are more revealing than the words that give it form, the spectator may yet find interesting freedom and breadth within the otherwise descriptive and wholly defined creatures of reason.

Because the reality of the theater resides in the spectator and not on stage, the stage itself can never be more than an approximation of the real world outside the theater. The more the theater suggests an essential reality, the further it moves away from a portrayal of that reality. Every aspect of the dramatic performance represents conscious stylization, not the least of which is its action. Once the living presence of the actor has been established, his action will not be so much physical (with a consequent emphasis stageward) as spoken, so as to transfer that action to the spectator. Before the existence of stage lighting, Shakespeare's words were able to illuminate the uninterrupted flow of time from midnight to dawn throughout the first act of *Hamlet*. Words used this way do not depict a fact, they synthesize its being; they are the words of a poet. There are also other kinds of words.

Examining the theater in the century following Racine's,

Diderot takes a critical look at a stage on which the actor has become a mere instrument of the written word, someone who faces the public, uses gestures in a limited and traditional way, and relies on the tirade rather than on stichomythy. This sort of stage is so obviously removed from everyday life that the spectator must provide even its first veneer of realism. Diderot no longer trusts the spectator to achieve that assimilation. He wants the actor to develop a greater power of suggestion by imitating outwardly the intimate proposition of his words. Thus he suggests that the stage be furnished with the apparatus of real life—including its speech, in form and delivery. Diderot hesitates on the portrayal of physical action, resisting as he does a wholly conventional stage gesture but evidently reluctant to abandon it entirely. As an art critic thinking about the stage, the literary canvases of Greuze come to his mind, evoking the ideal stage gesture (a thought that does the art critic more credit than it does the drama theorist): Diderot believes that the unfolding stage action might be sequences leading to such tableaux. And rather than universal types whose external features must perforce be lost (the latter-day puppets of Craig and Baty), he wants the particularization of well-known trades to be the recognizable faces of such feelings as the drama will convey.

It is interesting to note the hesitations of Diderot in regard to the stage action; they are an awareness of the limits to realism. Diderot knows that if he succeeds in simply bringing the street on stage, he will have merely eliminated the stage. There is another sign of this awareness—he realizes that his tradesfolk cannot talk plain shop without making a shop of the stage. As a *philosophe*, Diderot has a ready answer: the play will serve as a vehicle for the exchange of "philosophical" discourse.

But this awareness does not enable Diderot to foresee certain consequences of what he is advocating. The theater which he rejects, the one upon whose boards the actor merely serves a text, lends to that text the sensual dimensions of a human voice. It is understandable that he might protest against the overmechanization of this process, but it is curious that the sensualist in Diderot should not have perceived that there is little more any stage can offer as an inducement to the spectator. Alongside it, the props which he demands are feeble adjuncts with which to make the stage word human—if they are not simply detrimental. Moreover, when Diderot asks that ordinary and circumstantial people take over his stage, he is causing the stage focus to be shifted from the faithful portrayal of "sentiments" which he desired. Either these people will have to be more interesting than their particularization in order to attain credibility and significance (in which case their circumstantial nature can hardly be stressed), or that credibility and significance will be settled upon particularizing attributes and the play will be concerned with a delineation of surfaces. There is a difference in kind between the coal miners of Emile Zola and those of D. H. Lawrence. The first are more convincing as coal miners; they interest primarily historical sociologists. The second do not rely on the coal mine for their reality; their acceptation by the reader depends on traits that have little to do with their trade.

Lastly, Diderot fails to note that if characters who have little existence of their own are given words that will be equally pertinent in or out of their dramatic context, the actor becomes ancillary to a nondramatic statement. The stage action is then in danger of being limited to a more or less lifeless reading of didactic material.

When Diderot speaks of replacing *caractères* by *condi-*

tions (social situations), he is in fact speaking of lessening the people on stage—he introduces the notion of comedy. Comedy recognizes the existence of a man on stage; to a greater or to a lesser extent, that existence asserts itself whenever the actor has consciously stated his presence. "Interest" expresses the recognition of a human being. Even before the actor appears on a barren stage, the spectator will search that stage for comic signs, if the action is to be comical, for solemn portents if the action is to be tragic: the spectator awaits a human presence. Only if he does not expect any significance from what is on stage—if no *play* is to be given—will he casually note indifferent objects on it, whether props or people; he is detached. Once the play *is* given, only one stance approximates such detachment, the critic's. If the spectator should "come to think of it," any play will suddenly become an alien entity. The critic encompasses the entire action intellectually—he is god. What happens cannot touch him since he exists only as a mind, not as a human responding to a human presence. He is Oedipus after the final curtain; lesser wisdom cannot reach him.

Comedy acknowledges a man, but that man is not awesome. The spectator condescends to his existence; he looks down on him. Ultimately, this condescendence turns to contempt: the spectator laughs. Once the admirable hero is isolated because he has remained fixed in one form of a constantly evolving set of circumstances, he is likely to meet with the same fate—the melodrama becomes comical.

The dramatist may also strive consciously to elicit from the spectator the ambiguous response of laughter. To do so, he will strive to have the spectator retain his critical faculties by restricting his characters. The comic mechanism inverts the tragic. In tragedy, the stage synthesizes the spectator's aspiration; it represents the part of him that lies beyond his reach. In front of the comic stage, the spectator is allowed to show his contempt for a person in whom this aspiration never exists. This is the pessimism of comedy. It sees only the posturing of man, never the vision that gives a meaning to the posturing.

The comic playwright fights the reality of the actor. He must circumvent a source of sympathy, an area of recognition; he must neutralize the intimacy of an echo. Since the drama is principally spoken action, he may attempt to cancel the actor by substituting his own words for him; the actor then merely lends his voice to the author. In *The Importance of Being Earnest,* Oscar Wilde indicates precisely the "importance" which must be accorded to the protagonist —that of a linguistic pun. This sort of play remains exactly what it would be in a *salon,* an exchange of wit. It proceeds on an intellectual level. In the reciprocal understanding between spectator and stage—or, more properly, between spectator and author—it is very nearly possible to forget the interposed figure of the actor.

The Wildean comedy is usually termed "high comedy" because there is no person on stage to degrade it. Of all drama, it comes closest to ignoring the human aspect of the stage, and only in retrospect does the spectator realize that the human condition encompasses even these nonhuman figures. The Wildean comedy stands in contrast to the more habitual sort of comedy in which the character is a tangible quantity, but one deliberately debased in order to achieve laughter. This sort of character is difficult to create and unsatisfactory; bringing him into existence is an act suspended because he must never be allowed to exist fully. Part object and part human, his comic essence is constantly endangered. If he is too much an object, the spectator will remain indifferent; if he is too much like the spectator, there will be no laughter. The delicate balance for which the comic playwright strives is the attainment of only enough recognition on the part of the spectator for him to assert his superiority. The responsive emotions that are an instinctive link between man and man must be replaced by derisive ones that measure a man against a halfman. Instead of giving himself, the spectator must assert his difference.

The sensual properties of the comic type are thus reduced to a minimum. He is solid rather than sensitive—heavy, stubborn, hard. The action which he performs exists for its own sake and is of no consequence. His world is fraudulent and the spectator is aware of it (though short of turning critic, the spectator remains linked to that world by some human truth). He performs amid equally tangible objects: he and his world are material and massy and have only their visible significance.

Autonomy in the stage person, his suggestiveness, and his physical reality are invitations to the full being of the spectator. The spectator can laugh only from afar and when he realizes that the person on stage is of another kind. To avoid cases of mistaken identity, the author tries to retain control of the comic personage, for only in bondage is he functional —in contrast to the tragic character who escapes from the author to await definition by the spectator. But total control is impossible since (laughter being attainable only at the expense of that which is human) the part of the comic character that is necessary for laughter belongs to the spectator.

This fact has been noted by the comic authors, past and present, who have questioned the unsatisfactory nature of the comic creation. As these comic authors have been brooders and believers in the gloomy duality of man, it has meant to them that within the comic object the residual man is tragic. They have therefore been able to see that the comic character goes through the same systaltic motions as the spectator, except that his spiritual surges are limited in proportion to the greater assertion of his materialistic traits. But having detected that this conflict exists—even though in caricatural form—they have succeeded in imparting a guilty quality to the spectator's laughter, since in forcing the latter to recognize the identity of the object laughed at, the spectator becomes a self-conscious part of the negative forces that hem in, and frustrate the full existence of, a kindred being. This bitter laughter, which stresses the fundamental identity of laugher and victim, has been an effective statement of the human predicament and as such one of the significant contributions of the theater. It has nothing to do with the shallow and mechanistic "mixture" of genres; rather it develops out of the varying levels of the spectator's awareness that determines a subtle oscillation in his conflicting relationships to the stage. The rattle of this laughter is sometimes heard on Beckett's stage, and—to a lesser extent—on Ionesco's.

The stylization of the comic person deprives him of the freedom which the spectator recognizes as fundamentally his own. Furthermore, the comic person responds mechanically to imperatives that fall into categories, whereas the spectator will recognize as human only such responses as are wholly conditioned by the free surge of the vital organism (this postulate underlies *Le Rire*, 1900, by Henri Bergson). Characteristically, the tragic person is "free." Conversely, in the comic character, these traits suggest that he derives his essence not from a *person* but from a *type*. The French theorists for whom this concept is central to a definition of the comic personage (again Henri Gouhier as an example) point to the plays of their greatest comic dramatist, Molière, that are named for a general type rather than for a specific individual: *The Imposter* (*Tartuffe*), *The Misanthrope*, *The Miser*, and so on. But the type, no less than the person, must revert to the knowledge of a human being if it is to have any significance for the spectator. Even though a comic personage react automatically and previsibly, there remains the fact of his reaction which will be funny only inasmuch as it is a *human* act—ludicrous in consequence of its unsatisfactory development in human terms. In the particular case of Molière, the general types become quickly persons. It is for this reason that the curtain falls with such abruptness. The "general types" have begun living an existence—the spectator's—that defies all mechanical controls, including that of the final curtain which must thus come down by itself. The so-called "weak denouements" of Molière show him to have been a great dramatist.

The comic object of Molière's stage usually becomes a person. Only seldom is Molière gay; the dimensions of the human being on stage, and off, generally overwhelm the author. Man remains tragic, that is to say central, and thus the stage is set for the assimilative act of the spectator. In the tragic theater, there remains no objective clue to the work of art: it starts existing only when it has been wholly "taken in" by the spectator who empties the stage and frustrates the dramatist's ultimate control over his creation. Certain forms of theater may be viewed as reactions against this appropriation by the spectator (for example, the Wildean exchange of wit, the "admirable" drama, the simple flight from substance to surface which Nelson, in the work already mentioned, calls "the *fun* of play," and so on). Craftsmen of the theater, generally its intimates, have proposed yet another view of the play, wherein the theater itself is the sole performer. This stage is the primitive ritual ground in sophisticated habit. It is viewed as "absolute" (Mallarmé) and "magic" (Jean Cocteau, Eric Bentley, Jean Genet, and others), not because of the coercive presence of the living actor, but through the pre-emptory fact of its being.

This stage objectifies the work of art: admiration replaces assimilation. Deliberately, it shuns human concerns. The human presence that informs the object identifies itself and does not propose transmutation by the spectator. The stage mystery remains impenetrable to man and refuses his presence—the spectator is humbled. The stage belongs to the performing artificer; its spell is a euphemism because of this arrogation by the playwright.

Nevertheless, the magic stage operates within its means. It remains wholly inside the theater. It stands furthest from the didactic play that compels an alien mode upon the stage. No dramatic action is possible without its suasion; the actor himself is but a part of it. This sort of stage does not redefine the theater. It merely isolates one of its essential parts, that which belongs as well to the conjurer, the illusionist, and the necromancer. In eliminating man, it eliminates tragedy, but it also eliminates elements that are foreign to the theater —the intellectual and the critic. It sins only through restriction: it proposes means as an end. There is more to the theater.

There is always more to the theater; it is as free of limits as the one who defines it. Like that of the poetry to which Apollinaire refers, its challenge entails a constant struggle "at the brink of the unbounded and of what is yet to come." The double vision implicit in those words is also that of the dissatisfied playwright who feels the promise of stages yet undreamed no less than he feels betrayal in the unrealized possibilities of the stages attained. His attitude is shaped by these two visions, expectant in the first, frustrated by the second; and of his will to dare and to destroy is born the mood of the avant-garde.

Even as an act of faith and creation, the experimental play is aggressive when it remembers that it is also a protest. At such times, the very experiment it proposes trades an absolute freedom for the freedom to outrage; it reaches beyond its seeking in order to shock. Gouhier speaks of surprise as the preintellectual reaction to the dramatic act. Surprise in the theater, however, is significant only if it is the first intimation of an awakening, the instinctive animal response to a genuine intrusion of reality. When the play looks for shock as an ultimate for ethical or didactic reasons, it demands separation from the audience and frustrates the very motivity of the theater.

More than most, the consciously experimental play tends to become a personal assertion by the author who feels that his statement must dominate the more general truth which his characters may develop. However, his impatience and his anger work against his purpose. As long as the spectator is not given a stage world which he can accept, he is not able to translate the author's statement as an intimate formulation of his own and it remains for him—at best—an intellectual proposition. (And even though the play's irritation may be directed, as it often is today, against intelligence itself, the attack will be made as tractate, not as theater.) This failure to convince has the same causes as that of other intellectual propositions in the theater; a playwright like Brecht has often been made conscious of this. But whereas some of these direct exchanges between author and spectator (the comedy of Oscar Wilde, for example) offer themselves as an ultimate and a game, they fail as onslaughts that mean to impress their own validity.

The hostility latent in the protests of a young theater attacks all implications of humanity, in actor as well as spectator. A recognizable feature of postromantic avant-gardes has frequently been an expressed contempt for human dignity and human values and a characteristic brittleness, due to the absence of sensuality and sentiment (specifically human traits), which is intensified by a reliance on the symbol that replaces the person. It is noteworthy that the positive contribution of these theaters has usually been technical.

As such, the stage of the avant-garde never creates more than a brief stir. Either it dies in hopeless flights of which there remains only a meaningless clatter, or it is accepted as part of the current scene and dies in state. In the latter case, it often succeeds in knocking out dead parts of the former theater which it sometimes replaces with new modes of its own finding. The ceaseless redefinition of the stage and the repeated death of its revolutionary forms require a new avant-garde every few years, in spite of its insults, its noise, and its excesses. The youth and life of the ever-changing stage depend on it. And the spectator remains present, ready to instill his being into any part of the stage which he deems to be viable.

INDEX